VOYAGE AROUND EAST ANGLIA

Robert Simper

Published in 2001 by Creekside Publishing

ISBN 0 9538506 1 7
Copyright R. Simper
Printed by Lavenham Press

By the same author

Over Snape Bridge (1967)
Woodbridge & Beyond (1972)
East Coast Sail (1972)
Scottish Sail (1974)
North East Sail (1975)
British Sail (1977)
Victorian and Edwardian Yachting from Old Photographs (1978)
Gaff Sail (1978)
Traditions of East Anglia (1978)
Suffolk Show (1981)
Britain's Maritime Heritage (1982)
Sail on the Orwell (1982)
Beach Boats of Britain (1984)
Sail: The Surviving Tradition (1984)
East Anglian Coast and Waterways (1987)
Deben River (1992)
The River Orwell and the River Stour (1993)
Rivers Alde/Ore and Blyth (1994)
Woodbridge: Pictorial History (1995)
Essex Rivers and Creeks (1995)
Norfolk Rivers and Harbours (1996)
Thames Tideway (1997)
River Medway and the Swale (1998)
In Search of Sail (1998)
Family Fields (1999)
Rivers to the Fens (2000)

CHAPTERS

Introduction

This is the story of many different trips around the rivers and coast of East Anglia. It is also a voyage in time, because sometimes we look back into the past and see how things used to be. It is just a brief account of events on the East Coast, over a period of about fifty years, that have caught my attention.

So many people have moved into East Anglia that the correct pronunciation of many words has changed or even new names have been invented. Change is always inevitable, but I have endeavoured to record at least some of the true local pronunciations. Most of these place names were being pronounced long before they were written down. Now so many are in danger of being lost.

Many thanks for additional information on fishing from John Winter of Southwold and Dick Graham of Bawdsey and from Bruce Page on the Royal Navy at Shingle Street. On sailing barges I have to thank James Lawrence, Pat Fisher, Willie Williams, Barry Pearce and Colin Fox and on the Thames, Paddy O'Driscoll.

My wife Pearl has, as always, given me help on which direction to go. My son Jonathan has read it through and made good suggestions. That is not an easy task because I have a tendency not to listen to good advice. Diana McMillan has also edited and guided the finished work and my daughter Caroline Southernwood designed the map.

This book is really a follow on from *In Search of Sail,* about which several people said 'why didn't you do more about the East Coast?' Well now I have.

RS
Ramsholt

Sources of Illustrations: Eastern Daily Press, Jonathan Simper,
Colin Fox, Ron van den Bos, Jack Coote, Clive Southernwood, and Nick Rose,
Most taken by the author.

Opposite: The *Three Sisters* in the River Ore.

Chapter One

THE EMPTY COAST

It was six o'clock in the morning and drizzling when we lowered our gear over the Town Quay at Great Yarmouth and down on to the deck of the 22ft (6.70m) *Crangon*. Just ahead of us the shrimper *Boy Frank*, *Crangon's* sister ship, tugged manfully at her mooring ropes as the tide swirled under Yarmouth Bridge. These were the *Crangon's* old home waters, because Fred Symmonds had built her just up on the North River in 1957 and for some forty years had fished her out of Yarmouth. I had thought my cruising days were over when I sold my 35ft cutter *L'Atalanta* in 1993 and then for two years had shared my 18ft dipping lugger *Three Sisters* with my son, Jonathan. This had not really worked out because we each wanted to go sailing at the same time but with different age group friends.

'There is a Yarmouth shrimper for sale with an odd name, do you know anything about her?' Jonathan had asked when he came down to our cottage one morning. 'Sounds like the *Crangon*.' I replied and went on to explain that her name was Latin for the brown shrimp that she was built to catch. To cut quite a long story short, Jonathan bought her, John K expertly gave her a major refit and she was rigged out with the traditional Yarmouth Shrimper sloop rig with a loose-footed mainsail. My cruising career had resumed as a sort of ancient mariner and pilot, but I had still never been to the north Norfolk coast by sea.

Going down Yarmouth Harbour the rain intensified and Jonathan and Nick White, who had come along for the day, were struggling on the tiny foredeck to try and get *Crangon's* long bowsprit out. In the end we touched alongside a fishing boat at Gorleston, ran out the bowsprit and then headed around Bush Bend and out into the North Sea.

We turned north against the flood tide into Yarmouth Roads, the historic waters where a great fleet of sailing ships had once sheltered before making a dash up the coast to their next port. Perhaps I had read too many accounts of the ships leaving Yarmouth Roads. Of how in 1692 a sudden gale caught a fleet of two hundred colliers off the Norfolk coast and of these 140 were driven ashore with the loss of over a thousand lives. The only shipwreck I had ever seen had taken place here. In October 1980 the wooden brigantine *Luna's* engine had packed up when she was making for Yarmouth Harbour and she was driven ashore in the North Roads. Her people were saved, but the strong Baltic trader's hull had been reduced to driftwood in a few hours and all along the beach her timbers, spars, hatches and personal belongings were strewn in a pathetic tangle. Holidaymakers from the caravans had a wonderful time looting the wreckage in the time-honoured fashion.

The rain stopped and the sun came out as we headed northbound for Blakeney, some fifty-five miles away. I took this to be a good omen, if a trip starts well it will probably end well. The tide was still against us and we watched a lone coaster anchored at the north end of the Roads. She turned out to be a rather box-like *Hoo Venturer* and she swung round as we approached, showing that the tide had turned in our favour.

We hoisted sails, but kept the engine running. Once clear of Yarmouth there is no port that can be entered in bad weather until the Humber and the ship killing sand-banks lie off-shore. From the coast you can see the surf breaking on the Happisburgh (pronounced

The wreck of the jagt-built brigantine *Luna* on the North Beach, Great Yarmouth in 1980. She had been making for Yarmouth Harbour under power when the engine stopped and she was driven ashore and broken up.

Hais'bro) Sands where the seventy-four gun *HMS Invincible* met her end in 1801. She should have been part of the fleet of Hyde Parker and Nelson, who went on to win the battle of Copenhagen. Unfortunately she had been delayed when sailing from Yarmouth Roads and was trying to catch the main fleet. The young master and the pilot decided to sail the short distance between the banks off the Norfolk coast. Big mistake, the *Invincible* got ashore on the Happisburgh Sands with the loss of over three hundred lives.

On a calm July day such dramas seemed far removed from our little shrimper. We ate breakfast off the engine cover top as we hurried past Caister, knowing we were going over very shallow ground taking a short cut over the end of Caister Bank. We could see miles of sand dunes ashore with the red Caister lifeboat shed making a landmark to remember. At Sea Palling we sailed past the reefs, the latest man-made defences in the battle to stop East Anglia becoming part of the North Sea seabed. A chain of rocks, brought from Norway, had recently been put in lines to prevent the action of the waves from breaking down the sand dunes in a storm and flooding into the Norfolk Broads area. If the sea did permanently break through at Sea Palling, much of East Norfolk would have to be abandoned.

By Happisburgh the coast had changed to sandy cliffs, and there was still little protection against the sea here. These cliffs erode just as easily as the sand dunes. In the 1840s

The 22ft (6.7m) Great Yarmouth shrimper *Crangon* under full sail. She was built in 1957 as a motor fishing craft with steadying sails.

Jonathan and Nick White on the *Crangon* looking for the channel over Blakeney Bar, 1999.

James Forsythe, President of the Norfolk Wherry Trust, with Lady Beryl Mayhew at Wroxham at the hundredth birthday celebrations of the wherry *Albion*.

The wherry *Maud* sailing on Wroxham Broad in 1999. Linda and Vincent Pargeter on the right had taken eighteen years to rebuild and restore this wherry. The skipper is Mike Sparkes and the sailmaker, Mark Butler, is on the left. The wherry's sails were originally flax which were 'dressed' with fish oil, put on them as a preservative, but as rats found this very palatable, coal dust was mixed in to discourage them and this produced a black sail.

The Dunwich beach boat *Fred's Last* trawling, with Southwold in the background. 1998.

The 22ft (6.70m) Aldeburgh beach boat *Rachael Linda* launching off Aldeburgh beach, 2000. The Aldeburgh boats have a hauling-off line on a power winch to pull them through the breakers and another rope to the shore winch to pull them up the beach. The East Anglian beach boats always launch and come ashore bow first and are turned on the beach clockwise 'with the sun'.

fishermen formed a beach company at Happisburgh which operated a yawl, a powerful open East Anglian lugger, to salvage ships in distress. They had a watch house on the cliff and there were warehouses to store the coal, delivered on to the open beach by collier brigs. All this, and much more, has long since fallen into the sea as the tides have torn past the coast and steadily cut away any form of headland.

The cliffs rise steadily higher, usually with bare earth showing where the latest landslide has taken place. I was really impressed by the cliffs at Cromer, soaring up from the sea with green grass and the white lighthouse sitting on the top. I had no idea that such high cliffs existed anywhere in East Anglia. Another surprise was seeing the smoke from the steam engine on the North Norfolk Railway that carries tourists on a short journey along the coast. It was afternoon now and the mood aboard was very cheerful, as we all knew it was just another twelve miles to Blakeney.

But where was the harbour? We saw a white yacht sailing (the first we had seen all day), leaving the coast, she must have come out of Blakeney. Looking at the charts did not really help. Jonathan and I had each bought new charts and both of these were inaccurate. Later at home, when I looked at my Ordnance Survey map, it marked the entrance channel beautifully. I suggested we did not bother with charts and looked at the way the water was breaking on the sands to pick out the channel. This seemed to work, although it was worrying as we rushed in over the bar with angry little waves smashing all around us.

Suddenly it was calm and we were in the harbour, passing a colony of seals basking on the sands. Now we turned east to head for the little town of Blakeney, on the side of a low hill about three miles away. 'Where do we go now?' asked Jonathan.

To reach Blakeney, we had left the River Deben a couple of weeks earlier and made three hops up the coast. We had waited for good weather, taken a day off work, and then done another stretch of the coast. We had hopped from Bawdsey Haven to Southwold, then a short blustery and wet trip up to Great Yarmouth and finally the great day had come when we reached Blakeney. Getting there had been the thing and we had totally overlooked the fact that we had arrived on a small neap tide.

Thinking perhaps of Maldon or Woodbridge, I said 'well it's coming up to high water so perhaps we can just go up to Blakeney Quay.' Not a chance, we hit the hard sand, waited and floated, went on and then hit mud.

Jonathan did one of his rare impressions of Captain Bligh and announced 'this is my boat, so you can go off and find the channel.'
Nick White and I pumped up the inflatable dinghy and set off with a boat hook to do some soundings and find the Blakeney Channel. It took us some time to realise there was no channel to find, just an expanse of shallow water. The sand being torn off the cliffs of North Norfolk is steadily silting up these harbours. We kept moving up the harbour, but it soon became obvious that even in a craft drawing just 3 feet we were not going to get anywhere near Blakeney. Finally, we let go the anchor, abandoned our craft and in a rather inglorious fashion started to complete the final stage of our passage up to Blakeney in the inflatable. Progress with short oars was slow and we were glad when a returning local boat gave us a tow up the last part. Blakeney is a lovely spot, but it would have been quicker to have gone into Morston or a few miles further and up the easier channel to Wells.

Over a year later, on a September afternoon in 2000, Pearl and I returned to Blakeney Harbour, but this time not to the town, but to Morston, a village lower down the harbour. Although Morston dries like all the North Norfolk harbours, there is deeper water here than at Blakeney. In fact the eight Blakeney Harbour ferryboats, which are reputed to carry

100,000 people every year out to look at the seals on the sands off the harbour, have moved to Morston Creek. Pearl and I walked past about fifty people waiting on the salt marsh for the ferryboats to take them out to the seals. We climbed down into Charlie Ward's launch for a trip out to the new 45ft (13.71m) sailing barge *Juno* for an evening sail out of Blakeney Harbour.

The north Norfolk whelker *Knot* at Blakeney, 2000. She was still going out into the North Sea sea shell fishing.

During the launch trip out to the *Juno,* Graeme Peart pointed out the whelker *Knot* which was still going daily some 26 miles (48km) out into the North Sea, to shell fish. Most of these clinker whelkers, a development of the Cromer crab boat, were built just after World War II to operate out of Wells. Graeme had become so fascinated by the North Norfolk whelkers that he had bought two of them, the 26ft (7.92m) *Harvester* and the 30ft (9.14m) *William Edward*, the largest of the whelkers and planned to have one of these rigged out for sailing.

Once we were all aboard *Juno,* Charlie headed for the open sea, there is no time to hang about in Blakeney. We passed the seals having their photographs taken by the passengers in the first ferryboat. This is such a regular event that the seals take little notice of the boats. In fact you wonder if some are not members of actors' unions and are moving to show off their best angle for the cameras!

Charlie Ward had built a whole series of highly attractive and practical grp sailing boats to such an extent that most of the boats in the Harbour are either his Norfolk Oyster or

Gypsy class. The demand for new boats had tailed off, so Charlie pursued his next dream of getting a barge yacht built. Because the harbours are so shallow, a barge yacht seemed to be the solution to creating a sizeable yacht for North Norfolk.

Going over the Blakeney bar there are impressive breakers on the western sands, but with a local man on the wheel it is all very easy. I told Charlie about our difficulties the previous year to find the bar channel. He said he doesn't trust the buoys and because the channel changes so often he regularly walks the bar at low tide. Alan took the wheel now, while Charlie darted around the decks setting the gaff ketch rig, topsail and all. He couldn't stay still and was constantly moving around, discussing new ideas.

Thames spritsail barges were a commercial success in the Victorian era because winches were fitted which allowed two men to handle a large area of sail. A century later Charlie

The new steel 45ft (13.71M) barge yacht *Juno* on her moorings in Blakeney Pit. She only draws 2.6ft (.79m) making her ideal for the shallow north Norfolk harbours.

had pushed that idea a step further. The *Juno* has a mass of electrical gadgets. Even the leeboards are raised by electric motors operated by push buttons. I wonder what the old barge skippers would have said about that.

I was offered the wheel and the *Juno* rose and fell in the slight sea like a proper barge. She is probably the most successful of all the barge yachts which have been built. She happily pushed her bow up into the seas. As we turned back towards the sandy coastline, it was one of those magic moments you can get when sailing and everything was perfect. With the tide under her, *Juno* roared back into the harbour while the sun set over the trees at Wells and a full moon rose over the hills behind Cromer.

Chapter Two

SAILING PAST REEDBEDS

Graham Hussey and I peered at the edge of the water looking for some sign of how much the tide rose and fell. This was at Upton Dyke on the Norfolk Broads in 1989. For a week the Husseys had hired the 30ft (9.14m) grp sailing yacht *Seven Seas* while Pearl and I had the sister ship, *Windjammer.* The verdict of Graham and myself was that the tidal rise and fall was so small that it would not affect us much. We very quickly learnt that this was wrong. The tide has a great effect and the Norfolk and Suffolk rivers and Broads are a world quite apart from the estuaries of the East Coast.

To start with, we were quite cautious. We motored down Upton Dyke, quietly amazed at how narrow it was, as there was only just room to pass the craft moored along the bank. We went a short distance up the River Thurne and later walked up to the 'Lion' in Thurne. The local advice was that the North Rivers were the 'best bit of the Broads', so we decided to stay up there. Certainly, the rivers Bure, Ant and Thurne are most attractive, but they are also the most crowded. The River Yare up to Norwich mainly runs behind low cattle grazing meadows, while the River Waveney has a great feeling of remoteness about it as it winds its way up to Geldeston Lock.

The *Windjammer* had a very low cabin that we could just sit in, but for sleeping, safely moored up against the bank, the cabin top could be raised giving headroom. Next day the voyage began properly. As there were five members of the Hussey family, it was decided (by them), that one of them would crew with us each day. This worked well and we all met up for a meal together in the evening. Broads sailing seemed to be much more communal than estuary sailing, because you could moor up to the bank and walk along and have a chat with your friends.

Next day sailing began in earnest and we were most impressed with our craft. We could tack until the bowsprit almost touched the reeds and the *Windjammer* spun around on her central keel every time. We tacked up the Thurne to Potter Heigham (He'ham), where the huge yacht station has the air of a 1930s holiday camp. We had a brief stop to lower the mast to go under the narrow brick bridge. As I motored towards the bridge it suddenly dawned on me that tides did matter on the Broads rivers. It was nearly high water and there was a strong current sweeping us under the low bridge. Luckily, I caught the bridge dead in the middle and we shot under with a few inches to spare. However we heard a loud bang and a scream as the yacht following us struck the bridge with an impressive blow.

We sailed through the rural tranquillity across Heigham Sound and up to Horsey Mere. Here the North Sea is very close, visible across low-lying marshes, and the whole area has been flooded in the past when gales washed away the sand dunes which the Sea Palling reefs now hope to protect. The staithe here is peaceful, but all these Broads quays have been urbanised. There was neatly cut grass and fussy little paths that I suppose visitors expect to see in the countryside. The Norfolk wherry *Albion* left before us and her crew worked hard, quanting this 58ft (17.68m) long craft down the cut to the open Mere. Once on the Mere, up went their big single black gaff sail. This was heavily reefed as there was a strong October breeze coming over the marshes. We sailed behind the *Albion* and when

The Fisherman's Hospital at Great Yarmouth was built in 1702 and above the doorway is a plaque of a three-masted lugger once used in the herring fishery. In 1844 Yarmouth had 120 of these luggers and there were others at Sheringham, Cromer, Lowestoft and Southwold.

we left the Mere it seemed strange to be in such calm waters. The *Albion* is a double-ended craft built in 1898 to carry cargoes, which she did until the end of World War II. She was then rescued by the Norfolk Wherry Trust, who have proudly sailed her as 'the last Norfolk Wherry'.

After a peaceful over-night stop at Hickling we sailed back down to Potter Heigham, right down the Thurne and out into the slightly wider River Bure in a really stiff breeze. The two yachts were being handled quite differently. I am afraid that I resorted to using the engine, but Graham, who as a schoolboy had sailed on the Ipswich grain barges, insisted on not motoring. The *Windjammer's* crew sat in the pub at Ranworth while the *Seven Seas* slowly quanted up the cut from the main river to join us.

The next day the whole story was repeated. We sailed up the very narrow River Ant to Barton Turf. Although we had the tide sweeping us up, the number of motor cruisers on the river made tacking a nightmare. You just missed one when another great brightly-coloured box appeared and tried to dash across the bow. By How Hill I decided discretion was the better part of valour and dropped the gaff main and big jib and proceeded under power. We left *Seven Seas* having problems among the hire cruisers and proceeded up to Barton Turf, where we had a walk around the village. Later the *Seven Seas* arrived with her very pleased crew, as they had made the whole trip under sail. However they had had some adventures, Dan had fallen overboard while quanting and once, being unable to

Janet Harker, Linda and Vincent Pargeter at the relaunching of the wherry *Maud* in 1996 at Upton Dyke. The *Maud* had been sunk in Ranworth Broad and the Pargeters had her lifted out and spent fifteen years rebuilding her.

come about because of a hire cruiser, they had sailed into an overhanging branch and then hit a cruiser.

We then had a quanting race, easily won by the *Seven Seas,* up a narrow cut to Neatishead. Here the trees almost touched each other overhead and with a continual line of cruisers motoring past, sailing was impossible. The next good sail we had was down to South Walsham Broad. In the darkness we walked up to the pub in the village for a meal and it was here that Dan beat the local champion at pool, before we walked back to the yachts in the moonlight.

The following day we beat up the Bure to Wroxham, the unofficial Broads Hire Trade capital. As we went up river our two yachts completely disrupted the hire cruiser traffic. Most of the time we had four or five cruisers hanging around just astern of us waiting for a chance to dash past while another lot picked their time to come down. The hire boat skippers were nearly all very well behaved, in fact there was far better seamanship here than on some huge motor cruisers and speed boats on the coastal estuaries, who often thunder past leaving a scene of chaos in their wake. However I found it very wearing to have to constantly keep tacking, half expecting to hit some floating caravan at any moment.

After seeing so many grp hire cruisers, it was a delight to spot Peter Bower's three wooden wherries at their Wroxham berth. These were the 56ft (17.07m) pleasure wherry *Hathor*, which had the same hull shape as the trading wherry and the white wherry yachts, *Olive* and the 53ft (16.15m) *Norada*, which have counter sterns. The sail up to Wroxham had

Pearl sailing the *Windjammer* in Meadow Dike which links Horsey Mere to Heigham Sound, 1989.

been so tiring that even the skipper of *Seven Seas* was happy to motor back down to Horning in the rain.

On the final day, we walked up to see Colin Facey who was rebuilding the 59ft (17.98m) wherry yacht, *White Moth*. Launched in 1915, *White Moth* was the last of her type to be built and had spent many seasons as a hire craft before becoming a houseboat. Her rebirth was wonderful to watch and long after we had left the shed the strong sweet smell of newly sawn timbers remained with us. The last day of this cruise became an endurance test. It was raining hard and a strong wind roared across the bleak Norfolk landscape, making it bitterly cold. As we had paid for this day, we were determined to visit another village. We ended up huddled around a fire in a pub at Acle Bridge, reflecting that Broads sailing seemed to be largely a matter of cruising from pub to pub. Because of the hire trade, Norfolk Broads pubs give good value for money, although some, catering for the hirers, lean towards the 'karaoke Saturday Nite' atmosphere.

The pubs on the Norfolk rivers were a local institution long before the first boat hirers arrived. They have survived better than the wherries which led to their construction, but fortunately, just after the Second World War ended, a group of Norfolk people got together and formed a trust to save the wherry *Albion*. One of the prime movers in the formation of the Norfolk Wherry Trust, now the oldest of its type in Britain, was Lady Beryl Mayhew.

In 1974, while researching for a book called *Victorian and Edwardian Yachting,* I drove to Framlingham Pigot, just south of Norwich, where in a pleasant country house I met seventy-six year old Lady Mayhew. She was tremendously charming and helpful and we chatted about the Broads as they had been just before World War I. Towards the end of the afternoon she coughed slightly, an obvious signal, and the door opened quietly as an elderly maid brought in afternoon tea on a silver tray. Lady Mayhew belonged to a now forgotten breed of courteous country gentlewomen who saw serving the community as a duty.

In 1998 Pearl and I were invited to Wroxham Sailing Club to celebrate the *Albion* being one hundred years old. To my surprise and delight, the very elderly Lady Mayhew had also come down from Wimbledon to celebrate the occasion. She was in fact over one hundred years old by then and just older than the wherry that she had helped to preserve. One of wherry skippers there was Mike Sparkes, who had become involved with wherries after discovering that some of his ancestors had been wherrymen. We had sailed on *Albion* a couple of years before when Mike was skippering from Ludham, where the Norfolk Wherry Trust has a boathouse. Mike lashed the boat alongside *Albion*, so that the 15hp outboard on its stern could push us down the narrow Womack Water, but once we were out in the River Thurne the outboard was stopped and the big single gaff sail was set. The wherry's mast is stepped well forward so that she can point up into the wind, but we had not gone far when the river bent around to the east and we slowly came up head to wind.

To get the wherry to tack, Mike had the crew walking along the deck pushing the huge quants to force the bow around. Hardly had the sail filled when round she had to be pushed again until finally she came completely head to wind and they dropped the sail a little and quanted her along with the tide. It was not difficult to see why wherrymen worked up a healthy sweat and needed a pint. The wind eased off and we swept along, past the delights of the lovely little pub at Thurne and on down to Thurne Mouth where it joins the River Bure.

Here, the wind freshened and we reached along past the ruins of St Benet's Abbey out on the marshes. She was certainly no problem to sail with the wind, but I was told she was really too big for the Northern Rivers. She had been built at Oulton Broad in 1898 to work to a maltings at Beccles (does not this make her a Suffolk wherry?) and was the only carvel wherry built. The rest were clinker built in a tradition that the Anglo-Saxons and then the Vikings had introduced to eastern Britain. The return journey, with the tide, was made without problems and the wherry got safely back to Ludham. Providing you have a good crew who are prepared to work hard with the quants you can get where you want to go.

Pearl and I had made a long voyage, in Broads terms, when we joined the 56ft (17.07m) pleasure wherry *Hathor* in 1995. The Broads Authority provide a very good scheme. They charter Peter Bower's little fleet of wherries and then offer day cruises to the general public. We began at Acle Bridge where *Hathor*, built as a gentleman's yacht on the lines of a trading wherry in 1905, and the two elegant pleasure wherries *Olive* and *Norada* were moored. The passengers on the two pleasure wherries sat with a degree of comfort and dignity on the counter stern, out of the way of crew. On the more traditional pleasure wherry *Hathor,* we were confined to the tiny foredeck with its garden seat. We set off to sail some twenty-three miles down the River Bure to Great Yarmouth, then across the open Breydon Water to join the River Waveney and then down to the little village of Somerleyton.

When Peter was certain that all his wherries were ready, the hand winches came into action to hoist the great gaff sails and we headed off down the River Bure. It was a good Force 6 NE and progress was swift. Too swift for Peter, because we would arrive at Yarmouth before the tide turned. On the bend of the river at Ashtree Farm, where the Bure runs briefly beside the Acle Straight Road, the wherries were moored and we had a pleasant walk along the river wall. Then we sailed on through Halvergate Marshes, a vast grazing area, and because we were catching the full force of the wind Peter decided to go even

The 82ft (25m) spritty barge *Dawn* at the Woodbridge Tide Mill quay in 1987.

The *Dawn* from her bowsprit end in the 1986 Colne Match.

The 28ft (8.53m) *Sea Fever,* a ship's lifeboat that had been rigged out as a gaff cutter, on the beach for anti-fouling at the Rocks Reach on the River Deben, 1960.

slower. All the wherries had their masts lowered, which was easily done as they have huge counterbalance weights at the foot of their masts, and we drifted down on the tide for over five miles.

At Yarmouth there were two bridges to go under. The engines on *Olive* and *Norada* were started, but as *Hathor* did not have one at that time we drifted on happily, under the control of her very skilful skipper. On the last of the ebb the wherries came out of the Bure into the fierce tidal waters of Breydon Water. At once the mud anchors were let go and we all stopped. This was the wherryman's equivalent of rounding Cape Horn, and the trickiest part of the passage. In their trading days wherries regularly went down into Yarmouth Harbour, but it was always a dangerous business drifting down through the Haven Bridge with the full force of the tide. The *Albion* was one of the wherries which had struck the Haven Bridge and turned over and sunk, although they got her up later. To do this with a wherry loaded with passengers was every skipper's nightmare.

As soon as the flood tide started, up came the mud anchors. There was the crackling sound of the ropes running through the big wooden blocks as the gaff sails were hoisted to propel us across Breydon Water at speed. The boat hirers in their cruisers had a field day with their cameras as three wherries went past under sail. At the top of Breydon Water it was right for Norwich up the Yare and left for the Waveney and down towards Beccles. It was early evening now and the wherries hurried on through the much quieter river to reach Somerleyton seven hours after leaving Acle.

After Somerleyton, the Waveney winds away for many miles to Beccles and the navigation now ends at Geldeston Lock. In the distant past there had been wherry trade right up to Bungay. The wherry *Albion* was built in 1898 for the Bungay millers W.D. & A.E. Walker. The dykes leading up to the mills and maltings are now filled in and the area around the maltings has become housing.

Pearl and I seem to be 'doing' Norfolk in short trips and in 2000 we had another sail on Peter Bower's wherries. Again these wherries were on charter to the Broads Authority, but this time on short trips from Beccles. The name Beccles means 'beck meadow' and the town still stands by the beck, the Waveney, which winds its way inland through green meadows. It is a peaceful place compared to the busy North River leading to Wroxham.

Time had moved on again because the wherries were crewed, for their short trips down the river under sail, by the enthusiastic staff of the Broads Authority. Indeed two of the Broads Authority's ladies had qualified as skippers and were sailing the wherries, under Peter's ever-watchful eye, with great skill. All these wherries had by this time been fitted with engines. The *Norada's* electric motor made no noise at all, so at first I did not understand how we could suddenly head up into the wind and keep moving. We sat on the comfortable counter stern of *Norada,* surveying the scenery like a genteel Edwardian yachting party making a progress through the rural landscape. We enjoyed a brief trip past the red roofs of Beccles, a port far from the sea.

These tales of short trips on the Norfolk Broads began at Upton Dyke where we had returned in 1996 to witness the re-launch of the 60ft (18.29m) wherry *Maud*. This is an amazing story of quiet determination, because Vincent and Linda Pargeter had raised the sunken and partly rotten hulk of the *Maud*, a trading wherry built at Reedham in 1899, from Ranworth Broad where she had been one of the many craft sunk to stop bank erosion. Over the following fifteen years they had spent their spare time rebuilding the *Maud* and it was a great day in 1996 when she was lifted back into the water. After this it was over two years before she finally sailed again. No ship is ever too old to be saved.

Chapter Three

SANDY CLIFFS AND BAR HAVENS

When we left Lowestoft in *Crangon* on our passage back from North Norfolk, there were hardly any craft to be seen. Just one or two fishing boats were moving about on the horizon. On the East Coast the tide is everything and the trip was planned to make the maximum use of it. The tide was still ebbing against us when we shot out of the Harbour pier heads at Lowestoft. With only about an hour of ebb left we knew we would then have the whole of the flood, over six hours, to carry us south down the Suffolk coast to our mooring in the River Deben.

We ploughed south, casting our eyes at the coastal beaches as we went past. There was no sign of life on Pakefield beach, where we could see several small angling boats hauled up, nor was there any activity at Kessingland. We passed the sandy cliffs of Covehithe, which don't grow up with grass because they are constantly slipping into the sea. Because there are no coastal defences the coastline here has, since 1817, retreated 700 metres. Much of Covehithe Broad is now part of the North Sea, but an 800 AD Anglo-Saxon log boat, which had probably been used on it, came up in a Southwold boat's trawl.

Kessingland Beach End is not ancient settlement, because until the late eighteenth century privateers, the much feared Dunkirkers, used to raid the coastal shipping and towns in three-masted luggers. It was only after the Napoleonic Wars that the North Sea was safe enough for people to live near the remote coastal beach landings. The nineteenth century was the great heyday of the beach landings because hundreds of small sailing ships in the coal trade passed regularly, creating a great deal of work. The fishermen organised themselves into co-operatives known as beach companies. Each company had a lookout, where constant watch was kept on passing shipping, and 'yawls' (pronounced yolls) were used for salvaging sailing ships that got into trouble. There were beach companies all the way along the coast from Mundesley to Felixstowe Ferry. The sailors called the beachmen 'salvage sharks' and hated the sight of their sleek white yawls racing across the seas to prey on their misfortunes.

The double-ended clinker yawls were dipping luggers sailed by large crews. All the crews of the yawls helped to launch them or had a share in the company and received part of the salvage money. This salvage work supplemented the very meagre wages earned in longshore fishing and the yawls were the pride of every company. When the Royal National Lifeboat Institution began opening lifeboat stations along this coast they had a hard job persuading the beachmen to abandon the practice of racing off to claim salvage from the ships in distress and instead to concentrate on saving lives.

The RNLI had an even harder job trying to persuade the beachmen to put to sea in their rowing lifeboats. In fact they would have nothing to do with them and the RNLI solved the problem by introducing a special class of lifeboat, the Norfolk and Suffolk, just to be used on this coast. These boats were very similar to the old beach yawls because they were primarily sailing craft and had a two-masted dipping lug rig. They could beat them to windward, but they were not self-righting.

Between 1870-1925 some forty Norfolk and Suffolk lifeboats were built and a few of these tough old clinker sailing lifeboats have survived. The 47ft (14.39m) *Elizabeth Simpson*, built by Beeching Bros at Yarmouth in 1889 for Gorleston is laid-up at Wroxham, while the 38ft *St Paul,* built by Beeching Bros in 1897 and based at Kessingland until 1931, is now housed in Chatham Historic Dockyard. The *Alfred Corry,* built in 1893, is now at Southwold Harbour, in the lifeboat house that was built on the end of Cromer Pier in 1922 and shipped down by barge to Southwold in 1999. The *Alfred Corry* would have gone if it had not been for John Cragie, grandson of her original coxswain, who found her in 1977 as a rotting houseboat at Maldon. He has put in decades of work to get her preserved.

In 1937 Ernest Cooper, Town Clerk of Southwold and the first man to try to tell the story of this coast, called these men 'Storm Warriors' in one of his books. The men who crewed on these heavy clinker-built Norfolk and Suffolk lifeboats were longshore fishermen who were used to working off open beaches in smaller versions. In 1927, when Billy English of Walberswick started fishing, he once counted eighty-seven sailing 'punts' trawling off the town, each crewed by two men. The 'harvest' of the longshore punts was the autumn herring and sprat fishery.

In order to earn enough capital to buy his own boat, Billy English had gone away for sixteen weeks on a Lowestoft steam drifter. He then bought the 18ft (5.48m) *Maud,* an open Suffolk boat rigged as a dipping lugger, for £8. The Lowestoft fishing industry then relied on men like Billy, because it had two different fishing communities - the trawler men who lived in the town and went to sea all the year round, and the men on the herring drifters who came in from the coastal areas and villages just for the autumn season.

One of the great, unsolved mysteries of this section of the coast is the exact location of Sole Bay. In 1672, in a period when the English and the Dutch were almost permanently at war over the control of the North Sea, the Battle of Sole Bay was fought here. The English and French fleets were taking in stores from Southwold when Admiral de Ruyter arrived with the Dutch fleet and attempted to destroy the combined fleets. The two fleets fought themselves to a standstill and parted with no clear outcome. The location of Sole Bay seems to have been lost in the mists of time. The Ordnance Survey map marks Sole Bay as being just north of Southwold pier, but in 1672 this area would have been dry land.

The village of Eastern Bavents, once the most easterly point of Britain, was on a headland just north of Southwold, but this has completely eroded away. It is heartbreaking to know that between 1900-2000 two hundred acres (81h) have gone into the sea and virtually nothing has been done to stop this continuing. Southwold has only survived because of the pierheads to the harbour. The first of these were built in about 1750 and have acted as breakwaters at the harbour mouth, but they have had the effect of holding up the silt in front of the town. There used to be a fishermen's beach village at the foot of the cliff in front of Southwold, but a storm early in the twentieth century completely washed it away. In the 1930s breakwaters were built to hold the beach in place and protect the town on the cliff.

Serious sea defences on the Suffolk coast started after 1900 and were it not for these, half Lowestoft, most of Southwold and Aldeburgh and much of Felixstowe could well have gone into the sea. The money spent on sea defences in the twentieth century was a very good investment for the community, but unfortunately towards the end of the century officialdom tried to sidestep the problem by producing 'environmental reports', designed to convince the people living in Suffolk not to ask for cash for sea defences. To those sitting in their London offices it appears much cheaper for seventeen villages and towns along the Suffolk coast to happily slide into the sea forever.

The loss of Dunwich should have been a warning to later generations to fight for their right to protection from the sea. In the early medieval period Dunwich and its huge natural harbour was the principal port in East Anglia. That was until the great storm of 1347, when four hundred houses, churches and windmills were swept into the sea. With a quarter of the town gone, it never quite recovered. In 1677 the sea reached the marketplace and they sold the market cross. The sea must have moved inland about a mile this time and in 1740 a north-easterly gale lasting for four days finally swept away the last of the old town. With modern sea defences Dunwich could have been saved. It would have been a wonderful place to sail in to, a kind of 'Lavenham-by-the-Sea'.

The old sailors believed that in a storm, or when the tide turned, they could hear the Dunwich church bells ringing under the sea. Some fishermen would not go to sea if they thought they heard the bells, because it meant a storm was approaching. In 1856 Master Mariner John Day claimed that he always knew when he was approaching Sizewell Bank because he could hear the bells, and perhaps they really did ring when the churches first went under the sea and the legend lives on.

Going south in *Crangon* we did not hear any bells, but we were aware that we had sailed over the old religious capital of East Anglia. We passed the 20ft (6.09m) Dunwich beach boat *Fred's Last LT 436* trawling. The man at the tiller gave us a friendly wave. This high-sided Suffolk beach boat was built in 1979, and as her name suggests, was the last to be built at Lowestoft by Fred. Sadly, this type of clinker working boat is doomed to extinction because no more are being built. Russell Upson and his son Brian built a series of Suffolk beach boats in the eighties, ending with the *Sea Spray* for Eddie Strowger in 1988.

The only wooden-built boat to work off the beaches after this was the 20ft (20.06m) *Dodger LT 132* built by Frank Knights at Woodbridge in 1991. Phillip 'Dodger' Holmes had the *Dodger* built to work off the beach at Dunwich, going trawling for plaice and sole between April and September and fishing for sprat, herring and cod in the winter. It is not difficult to see why the inshore fleet is steadily declining. When Phillip Holmes started in 1964 they were regularly landing 100 stone of fish a day, but by 1994 this had dropped to an average of 20 stone a day.

Going past Sizewell, we could see the beach boats hauled up near the huge Power Station, a series of vast silent buildings which dominate this section of the coast. In the eighteenth century, isolated beach landings at Sizewell Gap were greatly favoured by the smuggling gangs. From here gangs of armed smugglers rode inland with tobacco and tubs of brandy, terrorising everyone they met on the road.

We swept around Thorpeness, just keeping off the broken water that was caused by the tide running over shallow ground. In Edwardian photographs a dozen luggers can be seen hauled up on a wide beach at Thorpeness. The remaining beach boat is *Shady Nook*, perched on the edge of the steep shingle, and she seldom goes out. There is a shallow patch just off the beach which can making landing difficult and the boats have moved away to Aldeburgh.

In the area behind the sand dunes it is just about possible to trace where Thorpe Haven was filled in with the tide, but from the sea the half-timbered holiday houses and the newer houses stand up above the beach. Thorpe was a fishing hamlet until the landowner Glencairn Stuart Ogilvie built his Edwardian holiday village and country club and renamed it Thorpeness. The early houses all had servants' quarters for nannies and maids, as Thorpeness was designed as a 'Merry England' holiday paradise for children. This was centred around The Mere, a boating lake dug between 1911-13, by hand, after the 1910 flood when the water ripped a hole in the grazing marshes. Many people who came here on holiday came back and settled in the area or returned here to retire.

Still going south with the flood, we could see the roofs of the town of Aldeburgh on the low shore, but there was no sign of any boats at sea off Aldeburgh beach. No doubt as it was late in the morning they were already back ashore and the fishermen were repairing their nets and retailing fish to the public. There was plenty of evidence of the Aldeburgh men's fishing grounds in the number of buoys with flags on them marking lobster pots and anchored nets on the seabed. There are so many nets on the seabed along the coast of the Suffolk that only a very lucky fish swims past them all.

We sailed close inshore to have a look at Aldeburgh and its beamy wooden boats hauled up on the beach. The story here is the same as at Dunwich. When Rodney Burns of the Aldeburgh Fishermen's Guild started fishing in 1969 the boats would have returned deeply laden with fish, but by the end of the twentieth century they were happy to get a couple of boxes of sole. One of the problems has been aggregate dredging off the coast. Suction dredgers working from Yarmouth and the Thames hold licences from the Government to take material from the seabed for the building trade. It is a sophisticated operation, with dredgers scooping up over a thousand tonnes in a few hours, but it leaves problems behind.

In the early 1980s one of the good fishing grounds off Orfordness was dredged for aggregate and has never recovered. The Aldeburgh fishermen complained bitterly about the loss of this ground, but the Government, which likes the revenue, refused to move the dredging licences to deeper water because it claims there is 'no scientific evidence' of longterm damage to fishing. After this, the dredgers worked off Southwold where there is a danger of them lowering the offshore banks. This would increase the size of the waves that can hit the beach and then cause a great increase in erosion. The Dutch realised the danger and stopped aggregate dredging off their coast in 1991. Instead they buy aggregate dredged off the East Anglian coast.

As we passed close along the Aldeburgh beach in *Crangon* we were again sailing over the site of a town. When the half-timbered Elizabethan Moot Hall on the sea front was built, it stood in the market square in the middle of the town, but since then about two streets have gone into the sea. This includes the house where the eighteenth century Suffolk poet George Crabbe spent his childhood. Crabbe witnessed a big storm and tide in 1779 when eleven houses were swept into the sea. He gives a heartrending account of breakers smashing down the roofs and knocking over the walls. Crabbe's best known work is *The Borough*, a grim tale of brutal fishermen, published in 1810. It was this poet who inspired Benjamin Britten to compose his first successful opera, *Peter Grimes,* which led him to return to Suffolk and start the Aldeburgh Festival in 1948.

Aldeburgh, a pleasant little town of up-market gift shops and expensive second homes, quickly faded astern as the tide carried the *Crangon* south. After this the coast becomes a low shingle beach extending down to the red and white lighthouse on Orfordness. The Ness, if you look at a map, is the chin of East Anglia, while Lowestoft Ness is the nose. As any boxer knows it's the chin that takes the most hammering and the North Sea has, over the centuries, given the Suffolk coast tremendous punishment. All this had a profound effect and it became an economic backwater. The lack of opportunity, outside of fishing and farming, forced people to leave. Those with money bought a passage to the New World, others walked to Ipswich and even London in search of work while the poor and orphans were sent off in wagons to the new industrial towns in the Midlands and the North.

The flood tide forced its way around Orfordness, kicking up an angry cross-sea, but it was peaceful when we reached Hollesley (Hoseley) Bay. We had passed from the open North Sea into the slightly more sheltered Thames Estuary. South of the Ness the offshore banks act as breakwaters so that it is rare for waves of over 25ft (7.62m) to reach the beaches, but when they do they eat away the foreshores equally as ruthlessly as they do to the north. From Aldeburgh south around the Ness the coast is very empty, just the hamlet of Shingle Street sitting precariously on the beach top, overlooking the bar at the mouth of the River Ore.

In 1810 Admiral Saumarez, fed up with the difficulties of operating a squadron of Royal Navy ships-of-the-line from Yarmouth Roads, persuaded the Lords of the Admiralty to find him another base. They had the shoals in Hollesley Bay buoyed so that the Royal Navy could use it as an anchorage. This was probably the beginning of Shingle Street, then linked to Bawdsey by a road along the coast, which needless to say has since gone into the sea. Shingle Street started as a shore base for the Royal Navy and then became an isolated fishermen's hamlet. The fishermen were mostly squatters who built their single storey cottages with driftwood from shipwrecks on the Ness. In the winter the fishermen and their families lived on potatoes and salted herring and whatever they could poach on the marshes. They were poor, but very resourceful people, fishing, salvaging and wildfowling and they even devised huge underwater spoons for taking coal out of the hulls of sunken colliers.

In the late nineteenth century Shingle Street stood inside the mouth of the River Ore. There were even yachts kept on moorings in front of the houses. Then, during a big storm in 1896, the river broke out to the north of Shingle Street and formed a new mouth. My first memories of this place in about 1950 are when the old river mouth was still there in the form of two huge lagoons. There even remained the hulk of the schooner *Rudolf,* which had been wrecked when entering the old river mouth, loaded with coal. These lagoons were all washed away and by 1965 the sea almost reached the houses, with gales pushing driftwood into their gardens. On a high tide the water percolated through the shingle under the houses and ran out on to the road behind. To save the hamlet, 22,000 tonnes of shingle was brought from Landguard Point and dumped in front of the Coast Guard Cottages. Both the hamlet and the highly productive land and marshes behind were saved by this wise expenditure.

The last boat to work from here was an attempt in 1986 by James Green to revive fishing with the Aldeburgh boat *Our Soles,* but the shingle was building up in front of Shingle Street making it difficult to launch boats. It extended so far that there were no boats left on the beach by 1989. By 1998 the Ore mouth and its shallow bar had crept south, almost to the position it had been a century before. This time the change was not caused by a dramatic storm but simply by restless movement of shingle, which opened up a new channel over the bar to the north. For the following year there were two shallow bar channels, the new and the old, then slowly the shingle closed the southern one.

The shingle appears to move, at both the Shingle Street and Deben entrances, in huge circles so that over a period of around fifteen years they go to the south and then move back north, but there are no hard and fast rules. The channels move mainly in devastating winter gales, but even in the summer the shingle is constantly shifting. Sometimes the gales push it into high knolls. I was told that once, in the 1920s, grass grew on the knolls at Shingle Street, then in other years the knolls were flattened and the shingle lay on the seabed just offshore. Some shingle is always escaping and moves slowly south until it finally reaches the training wall at Landguard Point.

In *Crangon,* with a powerful engine, we had no trouble crossing the Deben bar and ending our passage, but the entrance to this river can be a terrible place in an on-shore gale. The bar channel was opposite the golf club house and most people expected it to follow the pattern of the Shingle Street bar and break a new channel to the north near Bawdsey Manor, but it didn't. After the following winter's gale the bar had moved to its furthest southerly point ever, just opposite the Dip.

Unless you were there yesterday, it is never possible to say 'I know the Deben entrance', because it is changing all the time. Once in 1983 I agreed to take Chris Opperman and a radio crew on a trip up the river in *L'Atalanta* while they had a live broadcast on Radio Orwell. Passing Felixstowe Ferry Sailing Club at low tide, where I thought there was twenty feet of water, we suddenly hit a new shingle bank. I was suitably surprised and considerably embarrassed, but the broadcasters thought it made a wonderful talking point. Bless them for their discretion.

A short time afterwards there was deep water again off the Sailing Club, but this bank has returned. A great north-easterly gale early in 1996 sent huge waves rolling against the coast and the sea, because the sea defences had not been maintained, almost broke through Boat House Point at the end of East Lane to make Bawdsey an island. This gale caused a huge movement of shingle, a new knoll appeared off the Deben entrance and more shingle was pushed up into the Deben to recreate the bank off the sailing club.

Beach boats racing at Kessingland. The races for inshore fishing boats on the Suffolk coast started in about 1860 and the last race at Kessingland was held in 1948

Chapter Four

HERONS IN THE MIST

In *L'Atalanta*, the 35ft (10.76m) gaff cutter I owned for twenty-three years, I always slept in the coffin-like pilot quarter berth, partly because I liked it and mainly because no one else would sleep in there. In September 1971, at Snape Maltings quay, I struggled out of this snug, but cramped berth just after four in the morning, quietly pushed back the hatch and went on deck. It was totally silent that summer's morning. All around us was a thick blanket of mist that made everything damp on deck.

Bob More had already started to light the stove for a cup of tea. He looked at the mist, 'Are you going?' The previous day we had had a wonderful trip around from the Deben, but we had to leave on the early young morning tide, or we would have been there for twelve hours, until high water in the afternoon. Apart from the freshwater river running down from the top of the River Alde, the top of this estuary dries out completely. It is the most difficult channel on the East Coast. Between Snape and the deep water at Aldeburgh the channel corkscrews over a wide expanse of mud. The channel, at the top end, is just marked by withies stuck in the mud, while lower down there are buoys.

'Oh yes, we will go', I decided and started the diesel engine as Bob cast off. The big diesel sounded very loud, even with the engine just ticking over. We moved off into the silent wall of mist, only able to see about twenty yards ahead. Bob went on the bow pointing to the withies as he spotted them. Pearl and our young family appeared out of the hatch and then vanished back to their bunks.

It was a magic morning. As we moved quietly down river, we spotted not only withies, but herons feeding by the channel. Some flew away, but several gaunt grey birds ignored us and stood in the still water watching for the unaware fish, which would provide their breakfast. By Iken Church the mist had started to rise. The Church stands on the site, or very near to an Anglo-Saxon monastery and with the mist blotting out the few modern buildings on the adjoining countryside the centuries slipped away. I half wondered if some hooded Saxon monks might appear on the foreshore and push off in some little clinker boat for a bit of fishing. In luggers we still speak of sailing 'amonk', basically a sloppy set of the fore lug, perhaps harking back to the days when monks sailed their own boats, but fishermen thought they were a bunch of amateurs.

After Iken Church the channel twists back on itself and you find yourself looking back up the Alde at the Victorian red buildings of Snape Maltings standing proudly in the marshes. The opening of a concert hall and shops at Snape Maltings in 1967 had a profound effect on architecture in eastern England. Before the Snape Maltings conversion, all the redundant industrial buildings had been pulled down. The same was true of old cottages and farmhouses, which were smashed down in part of the slum clearance schemes. Snape Maltings made people realise that old buildings often had great character and could be adapted for a new role. The next step was to actually incorporate traditional features in new buildings. This came a full circle when in 2000 the 'Plough & Sail's' new restaurant at Snape was built in the style of the adjoining Maltings.

In the old 'Plough & Sail' the malsters used to sit in the tiny rooms and amuse them-

The *L'Atalanta* sailing past Bawdsey cliffs on the way back from Snape to the River Deben in the autumn of 1971. Normally one does not get photographs of one's own boat, but Jack Coote took this photograph as he sailed past.

selves by growing barley, kept watered with beer, in the cracks in the wooden tables. The 'Plough & Sail's' new restaurant is a far cry from the old working man's drinking den.

Snape quickly vanished from view as we turned into Long Reach past the Black Heath Mansion. The ebb was under us now and progress speeded up. The tide was running hard around the Cob Island, a patch of saltings off the old brickworks. We had been up this way many times and every time Cob Island seemed to get smaller.

At Slaughden we let the anchor go and went below for a civilised breakfast, seated around the cabin table. This bend of the River Alde just below the town of Aldeburgh can be a bleak, windswept place, although the keen racing people of the Aldeburgh Yacht Club enjoy this ever present source of breeze. On that fine autumn morning many years ago we winched up the anchor and reached down the River Alde with a faint breeze.

Above Slaughden, particularly above Iken Church, the Alde is one of the most beautiful of East Coast rivers, but below, it simply runs between two river walls. It is believed that in the Roman period there was as much as a mile of coast in front of the present town of Aldeburgh. Around Slaughden's Martello Tower a little Roman and a lot of medieval pottery has been found. There is no pottery after the fifteenth century. Presumably a village off Sudbourne Beach went into the sea at this time, while the Alde to the north was growing as a centre of population. The ships for Aldeburgh then came in at Thorpe Haven and up to Thorpehithe at the northern end of the town.

Some time around 1542 Thorpe Haven became closed by shingle moving south and the merchants of Aldeburgh established a new southern wharf for the town at Slaughden on a narrow spit of land between Aldeburgh and the Lantern Marshes. To call Slaughden a port is probably too grand a word. It was just a couple of quays, a dock, a shipyard, a row of houses and the 'Three Mariners Inn'. The last well smacks, which kept their catch alive, in the North Sea cod fishery, sailed from Slaughden. Grimsby gave up well smacks in the 1880s, while Slaughden, which could not raise enough capital to buy steam vessels, went on out of desperation until 1914. There was poverty in Aldeburgh in the late Victorian period and to try and generate employment shopkeepers and tradesmen clubbed together and bought a smack for the cod fishery, knowing this would find employment for at least a dozen men through the summer.

They had less luck keeping the sea out, as it eroded away the shingle strip of land on which Slaughden sat and one by one the houses fell into the sea. In the 1930s there were Aldeburgh fisherman who had trawled over the site of the houses where they were born. Aldeburgh would also have gone into the sea, at least up as far as the Town Steps, if it had not been for a sea defence programme started in about 1948. Since then the beach has been made up and one is grateful to those forgotten committee members who voted for the cash to keep this part of Suffolk from going into the sea. The sea did break through at Slaughden in 1953, and would have again in 1988, if it had not been for the very wise, and very hard fought for, placing of stones in front of Slaughden beach.

On the right, behind the river wall, lay the great open area of Sudbourne Marshes. These marshes, like most of those along the East Coast estuaries, were ploughed up after the 1953 Floods. Environmentalists decreed this, but when much of the Sudbourne Marshes were returned to grass everyone was surprised to find that bird numbers fell by a third in three years. The truth is that wildlife needs farming, because growing crops or those left abandoned after harvesting is a major source of food. When Outdoor Pigs became a popular agricultural practice, with a free supply of food on the ground, the number of gulls nesting on Orfordness doubled to 1500 pairs. Some people in wildlife management believe that it is not the use of sprays that are harmful to wild life, but the EEC regulations forbidding birds to enter places where grain is stored. Another source of winter food is lost by the modern practice of ploughing up corn stubble, which rob birds of their food supply over the winter.

Below Aldeburgh the River Alde can't be called attractive, just a narrow channel between two river walls, but Orford, with its castle and church in the background, is a real little gem. A complete nineteenth century port, all now changed to residential use, but the quay, merchant's house and coal warehouses are all still there. On *L'Atalanta* during that trip the wind dropped just as we reached Orford and the ebb took us into the bight of the river off the Quay. The engine had to be started quickly to stop us from being swept into moorings.

On this trip we decided to stop in the Butley River to give the flood tide time to increase the depth of water over the bar at Shingle Street. In a light breeze we ghosted down the Gull behind Havergate Island. Havergate, a walled marsh island, was formed in the reign of Henry VIII when Orfordness extended further south, forcing the River Ore to cut a second channel. Havergate was once a parish in its own right, with a resident population. The marshes used to have furrow ridges, showing that the island was once under plough and had grown wheat. When Harry Fiske, who farmed at Bramford, just outside Ipswich, owned Havergate before 1914 he used to send his cattle down here to graze for the summer. The first day they were walked as far as Melton, where they spent the night in a meadow near the church, then the drovers walked them to Orford where a huge punt took them across the Gull to Havergate.

A shingle Knoll on the bar of the River Deben in 1996. Yachts running ashore on the bar used to be a regular occurrence and gave the Felixstowe Ferry fishermen a nice sideline in salvaging, but echo-sounders and powerful engines have made the Deben bar less of a problem.

Around 1930 the people of Orford got some amusement when a commercial traveller, who had been told to visit every parish on the coast, arrived on Orford Quay and asked when the next ferry down to Havergate went. The two families in these cottages used to row across once a week and walk up the river wall for supplies from Orford.

In the Second World War the whole of the Suffolk coast became a military zone. The beaches were mined and then lined with barbed wire while on the high ground, just back from the coast, there were anti-aircraft guns, searchlight units and army camps. Because of the threat of invasion, people were moved away and Havergate became one of the places that was abandoned. At some time, while the war went on above, avocets, which had not nested in Britain for about a century, returned to nest at Havergate and Minsmere.

Conservation has a good record on the Suffolk coast and there is no real shortage of bird habitat. The combination of the work of the bird empires and some of the farming community has brought back avocets, marsh harriers, brent geese, otters, and even stone curlews have made a slight comeback. It would be a great mistake to lose all this progress by abandoning sea and river defences and letting the coast slip into the sea. Conservation starts with protecting the land. After all, there is no shortage of sea, it covers two thirds of the world's surface, it is land that both humans and wildlife depend on for their existence.

Because there is no natural protection, the Suffolk coast is highly fragile. To destabilise the coast by abandoning any sea or river defences is highly dangerous and could result, over a long period, in all the seventeen coastal villages and towns going into the sea. This coast needs a long-term policy for keeping back the sea to protect people's homes, farm-land and bird habitat. Once land has gone there is simply no way to ever replace it.

It is strange that in 1971, when we set all *L'Atalanta's* sails, including the topsail which always managed to foul up somewhere, and took several goes to get up, we had never heard of The Environment. Nor had we ever heard of Global Warming, although we still had just as much bad weather and the problems with erosion were much the same.

As we sailed back along the coast to the Deben in the weak sunlight on a pleasant autumn afternoon, the problems of the world at large seemed remote. Whether the topsail was pulling properly seemed to be far more important.

Orford Quay in 1965. A complete small Victorian port.

Chapter Five

END OF A SECRET

The River Deben is too pleasant for its own good. The tidal section only covers about seven miles, between Bawdsey Haven and Melton, but because it is so attractive it is packed with boating activity. I don't know how many times I have been up and down this River Deben. As a very small child I went on the river before World War II, but to my great regret I remember nothing about this. Since 1946, when my uncle acquired the Shingle Street fishing boat *Lassie*, I have spent as much time on the river as possible. Again, I can't say which has been the best sail, but I do know the worse one.

In October 1991, Pearl and I thought we would have one of our favourite Saturday trips by sailing down from our creek to Felixstowe Ferry to have a fish and chip meal in the unique café there. We went in *Pet*, the 15ft (4.57m) open dipping lugger that we had rescued from Thorpeness beach ten years before. *Pet* had been the last Suffolk beach boat to be worked under sail. Until about 1967 Mr Wilson used to go off the beach in her to haul in his lobster pots. It was not a long trip and he used to hoist the sail or use an outboard for the short distance, depending on the weather.

When I had asked about the future of this dilapidated craft I was told that she was going to be put on the November Fifth bonfire, but when I then asked to buy her she suddenly became 'quite a useful boat which was going to be used again'. Anyway, we did buy her and she was rebuilt at Frank Knights' yard in Woodbridge. My aim was to restore a local craft and sail her in the traditional manner.

The sail down to Felixstowe Ferry was slow, because there was only a light S.E. headwind and we were mainly drifting on the ebb tide. We towed a dinghy as the tide was ebbing, because we would have to anchor off at the Ferry. Anyway, we reached the little fishing hamlet of Felixstowe Ferry, crunched across the shingle to the café and enjoyed the deeply fried fish and chips. As we walked back, the low autumn sun was setting over the river and I remember remarking 'well, the flood tide is just starting so we should run back before dark.'

As we climbed into *Pet* the wind suddenly went round from a slight S.E. to a strong N.E. and increased in strength. With the tide under us we beat out of the yacht moorings, but the wind was now so strong that we were forced to anchor and put in two reefs in the forelug and mizzen. All the time the wind was increasing and although the tide was with us, everything else was against us. Our progress was slow, because even in a small estuary like the Deben a gale force wind puts up angry little waves and these were buffeting away at the *Pet* and her dinghy astern. As we had no centreboard we often had to row her round on each tack and then re-hoist the forelug.

To make matters worse, heavy rain showers started coming down river as it got dark. Our voyage round Green Point turned into a miniature version of rounding Cape Horn and as we turned into the Ramsholt (Ram's Holt) Reach it was not much easier. We were charging back and forth across the river at speed, with the white shapes of moored yachts suddenly appearing and disappearing through the black and the rain. The near misses were worrying. It took us three and a half hours to cover just two miles and by that time we were losing the strength to row the lugger around.

Finally we gave up when we were able to sail her straight on to the mud in front of the Ramsholt 'Arms'. The lights from the front bar played on the mud and Pearl and I sat there, soaked and exhausted (we had not had time to put on oilskins). Feeling excluded from that place of warmth and safety I threw the anchor into the mud and we set off to walk home across the Dock Marshes and up the hill past the isolated Saxon church in the total darkness. Sometimes the best bit of sailing is when you stop.

The following day there was a lovely autumn sun shining and we gently ran back home. Because of the difficulties of this trip I made sure that when we had the *Three Sisters* rebuilt at Woodbridge three years later she had a new reliable engine fitted.

The waterfront at Woodbridge at high water is usually a scene of great activity as boating people make use of the brief appearance of the water. At low water ,Woodbridge waterfront is a peaceful place. The yachts sit on the mud and the ducks and about twenty swans mill about on the shoreline hoping to get tit-bits from people having their picnics. There used to be a ferry across the River Deben and I set out to find the old Woodbridge ferry landing hards. On the mud flats in front of the Tide Mill the rotten stumps marking this ancient crossing place were just visible. In about 1872 these hards had been abandoned and new low water hards were built slightly further down river. The hard on the Sutton shore had little effect on the river, but on the Woodbridge shore it had the effect of slowing down the tidal stream, so that it was constantly silting up.

The ferry at Woodbridge used to work every day of the year, except for Christmas Day, and was a profitable venture until just after World War II. After this, people heading for the Wilford peninsula found it quicker to go by bus or car. Woodbridge had been given the ferry right in 1919, on the understanding that they would run it for ever as a service for the community, but it became unprofitable in the late 1940s. Woodbridge Urban Council decided to get an Act of Parliament to allow them to close the ferry, but Mr Pelly, who lived at Ferry Farm, Sutton said his employees in Sutton still needed the ferry and fought against the closure all the way to the House of Lords. The goodly Lords in their great wisdom ruled that Woodbridge had to continue to operate the ferry.

Local councillors were far from happy with this outcome, but the landing hards and shelter were repaired and the former barge skipper, George Skinner, was employed as a ferryman. When George died in about 1969, Woodbridge quietly forgot about the ferry, which by then was very rarely used.

In 1984 I was asked by the Sutton Hoo Society to organise the reopening of a ferry across the Deben at Woodbridge so that people could cross and walk up to the archaeological dig which was taking place on the Sutton Hoo Anglo-Saxon ship burial site. Once we had made the intention of restarting the ferry public, one councillor, who had remembered the expense of trying to close the ferry, said that it would only be restarted over her dead body. Fortunately we managed to achieve the restart without going that far!

The first thing I did was to go and talk to Frank Knights, the boat builder down on the Ferry Quay. The truth was that without Frank's help nothing got done on that part of the Deben. Anyway he, like many other people in the town, had a soft spot for the ferry and was very helpful in its reopening.

That autumn Andy Seedhouse lent us two boats, and to test whether anyone was still interested in the ferry we offered to run a free service one Sunday afternoon. We operated it for two hours either side of high water and 120 people were ferried across the river. The publicity from that afternoon led to the gift of money from an anonymous elderly businessman, who had fond memories of Woodbridge, to buy a boat to start the service.

RS in the *Saxon* after delivering the first paying passengers across the Deben after the restart of the Woodbridge Ferry, 1985.

Following this, the final piece of the jigsaw fell into place when the Suffolk Coastal District Council, holders of the ancient right to operate a ferry at Woodbridge, gave me the right to restart it.

We got off to a good start and I think we ran the ferry at the weekends for about five summers. The problem was that the world had changed. In the old days the ferryman had a boat and a 'flat', a punt in which he pushed the passengers across the river at low water. None of our ferrymen were in the least interested in either rowing or using a flat. The Sutton Hoo Society first bought the *Saxon,* an open boat with an outboard, and then the slightly larger *Clog,* with an inboard engine. There was only high water at Woodbridge during the day every other weekend, but the public could not understand this. People would turn up when the river was just a vast expanse of mud and demand to know where the new ferry was running from. Eventually they gave up coming and the ferrymen lost heart because they were not getting enough work.

Some weekends I ran the ferry myself and it obviously gave pleasure to visitors, although we had to drum up trade from people walking past. Pearl was very good at encouraging people into believing they needed a trip across the river, while I operated the small boat.

Since childhood I had been fascinated by small boat handling. This passion was fuelled when I was nine and won a prize at school 'For Trying'. The prize, a book token, resulted in the purchase of Arthur Ransome's book *Secret Waters.* I had never voluntarily read a book of any description before, but I started to read this one and became totally engrossed. It was about the adventures of a group of teenagers who went camping on Horsey Island in the Walton Backwaters. It changed my life and I became an avid reader and passionate about pottering in small boats, but I had never been right around Horsey Island.

We had been into the Walton Channel many times and once went right up to Beaumont Quay, but what lay behind Horsey Island remained a mystery to me. Some fifty-four years after reading *Secret Waters* I decided that I must finally see this little area of the East Coast. There were only a few days in the summer when the tides would be favourable to go the fifteen miles from the Deben to Walton Backwaters and back in a day. Every time I planned to go, it was either bad weather or I was busy at work, but in early September 2000 everything finally fell in to place.

Nick Rose, who had read *Secret Waters* as well, was also keen to circumnavigate Horsey. At dead low water we cast off the *Three Sisters* mooring to head down river towards the sea. The Deben bar was well to the south in the year 2000 and the winter gales had left the shingle knolls flat. The incoming tide was already pouring over them when we reached the entrance. Ahead, the channel into Harwich Harbour, gateway to the Port of Felixstowe, was empty, but there were two faint specks on the horizon. By the time we reached the edge of the Harwich channel the first speck had become the commercial ferry *Dutch Trader,* which was pushing a wall of white water under her bow as she ploughed into Harwich. In our tiny open boat we had great respect for these monsters and we hung about, waiting for the second ferry to go, and two more to come out, before we dared dash across the channel towards the Pye End buoy that marked the entrance to Walton Backwaters.

The Russian 4-masted barque *Krusenshtern* passing Landguard Point, 1997. The art of maritime photography is largely being in the right place at the right time. In this case we were sailing out of Harwich in *Crangon* as this training ship left.

RS and Pearl aboard *Sea Fever*, returning from a cruise to the Essex rivers in the autumn of 1961. The rainbow is ending on the four pylons of RAF Bawdsey.

Tony Judd's 30ft (9.14m) *Alice & Florrie* was built with a centre-board by S.J. Peters at Southend in 1905.

The bowsprit barge *Portlight* in the Sea Reach in the 1996 Gravesend-Harwich Passage Race. The *Edme* won in the record time of six and a half hours.

Aboard the spritty *Memory* in the Pin Mill Barge Match, 1964 with the white sails of the *Maid of Connaught* astern. The *Memory's* mainsail is a flax sail dressed with traditional red ochre.

A few weeks earlier all the East Coast sailors had been deeply shocked when a yacht, crossing from the Netherlands, had simply vanished in the North Sea. A few days later the bodies of some of her crew had been found near the Friesian Islands. That clear summer's day we clearly saw all the ships moving at Harwich, but we did not hear their engines, even though we were very close to them. I suppose that out in the open sea at night, or in mist, a big ship, and there are enough of them, could come up astern un-noticed and go right over a yacht before it had time to get out of the way.

A couple of miles on and we were in the Walton Backwaters, a wide muddy bay dotted with marsh islands. The main channel, Hamford Water, cuts behind the islands and eventually peters out in a muddy creek at Beaumont Quay. That day we were not going to the head of the Backwaters, but took the 'second left' channel into Kirby Creek, to go around behind Horsey Island. It was half tide and we quickly slipped up Kirby Creek. On our starboard side was Skipper's Island, sadly long flooded, although trees on high ground survive. Eight seals were basking on the saltings and watched us with mild interest. After this we passed into Horsey Mere, behind the island, and as it was so shallow we could see the bottom.

Soon we were passing over The Wade, a road still used at low tide to reach Horsey Farm. We moved forward slowly, but the prop began to churn up black silt. Ahead, a small boat approached us from Walton. I steered towards it but Nick, who was standing in the bow and using the boat hook as sounding pole to show me where the deep water was, claimed we only had about a foot of water below us. The man in the other boat wore a red neckerchief and, as I thought to myself, 'only Jim Lawrence wears a red neckerchief', to my surprise, I realised that it actually was the famed Brightlingsea sailmaker.

Jim and Pauline Lawrence exploring behind Horsey Island, Walton Backwaters, 2000.

I had first meet Jim Lawrence forty-four years before, when he skippered the sailing barge *Memory* which was in trade. In the early 1970s Jim took up sailmaking and since then all our sails had been made in the Lawrence sail loft. We were both surprised to see each other and it turned out that Jim and Pauline Lawrence had not been behind Horsey before either. It was a bit like Stanley meeting Livingstone in central Africa in 1872; life is full of pleasant surprises.

Our little expedition ended as we passed the yachts on the pontoons off the yacht marina on our way to the Walton and Frinton Yacht Club to go ashore for a drink. I was glad that I had not seen Horsey Island when I read *Secret Waters,* as a boy. It does not quite live up to the romantic image. Arthur Ransome did well to spin a yarn to make these low islands and wide expanses of mud become places of great excitement.

The steel spritty barge *Xylonite* off Harwich in 1985 with the *Portlight* and *May.* The previous winter the *Xylonite* had a new bottom and new masts and gear which, because racing had become so important, were larger than the ones she had when trading until 1957.

Chapter Six

THE LONGSHORE HERRING

It normally takes us about an hour, under power, to go from our Deben mooring out over the Bar and into the open sea for our annual herring trip. In 1997 we were in my boat, the 18ft (5.48m) *Three Sisters*, which was rebuilt at Frank Knights' yard on the end of the Ferry Dock, Woodbridge. A dipping lugger, *Three Sisters* is a Suffolk beach boat built in 1896 at Thorpeness. We had found her as a rotting hulk and asked Frank Knights to rebuild her. All of the original hull was oak and some of this went back into the new hull, while the oak for the new keel came out of a Suffolk Seed Stores warehouse that had been pulled down. The new forefoot was of grown oak and the thirteen planks aside were sawn from 120-year-old Norfolk larch.

I had been very keen to retain the original hull shape as near as possible. The bow had a very fine entry into the water, so that she could be rowed easily, while further aft she filled out quickly so that she would rise with the seas. The Suffolk boats were launched bows first, so they had to have a bow that made the boat ride up on the incoming sea. The men on the shore pushed them off with the long mizzen 'outlinger' (outrigger) at the stern. Although she was built of wood in a traditional way in 1994, she was actually cheaper than a grp class boat of the same size would have been.

I wanted her to remain a traditional local boat and stuck to the dipping lugger rig. To be honest this is not a practical rig for beating to windward in a narrow estuary, but this can be overcome by using the motor. The considerable advantage of the dipping lug is that when you do motor or work nets there is no boom to get in the way.

It is the element of surprise that makes fishing interesting, never knowing quite what is going to happen. On one of our recent trips at night we found the nets were full of small bass and codling. We dutifully threw these back, until 'AJ' pointed out that there was something in the water just behind us. We shone a light and there, a few feet away, was a seal. He looked very happy and must, even in the dark, have been catching the fish we had tossed back into the river. He did not get any more!

This particular trip was in November 1997, when Mike Smylie had joined Jonathan and myself. Going down the Deben under power there had been a thick fog and I was not actually sure whether to go out to sea, but as we left Bawdsey Haven it was clear. It was high water and we shot the three nets across the tide to try our luck. It is said that herring swim into the wind, while sprat swim with the wind, which means that a north-east breeze is a 'herring wind' when they come inshore. On this particular day there was very little wind and we simply had no idea whether there were any fish in the sea at all. We drifted past the low cliffs of Bawdsey but there were so many buoys marking nets hanging to the seabed that we had to start the engine several times to haul our drift-net clear of them. In between times we sat in the bottom of the boat drinking tea from a flask. Once one of the powerful fishing boats from Felixstowe Ferry came over to have a look at the curious sight of a boat from the nineteenth century riding to nets with the mizzen set. They must have been convinced that we were not a serious threat to the European fish stocks, and left.

It is a great pity that boats can't talk, because *Three Sisters* might have been able to tell

The *Crangon,* entering the River Ore at Shingle Street in June 1999. In the distance is Boathouse Point, East Lane and we have come in through the channel along the beach, this channel was closed by the shingle in a SW gale in November 2000 and people could then walk across to the Knolls.

us about these waters a hundred years ago. Sometimes when the fishing was poor, or the bank in front of the beach made landing difficult, the Thorpeness men used to sail down the coast to make their base at Shingle Street. One boat would be hauled up on the beach there, and turned over for them to sleep under, while the other boats were used for fishing or to sail the catch up to Woodbridge to sell.

Once, years ago, in the Sailors' Reading Room at Southwold, a retired fisherman told us how, as a young man, he had been out in the beach 'punts' when a sudden north-easterly gale came screaming down out of a clear blue sky. Very few of the boats were near enough to make the beach and none of these open luggers could beat against the gale. In the huge seas the Southwold men sailed for their lives around Orfordness and managed to make their way up to Orford. Here they hauled their boats up on the beach and lived under the sails until the weather had cleared enough for them to sail home.

We had nearly drifted down as far as Shingle Street when we decided to haul in the nets. Mike, who has a small mobile fish-smoking house which he takes around to festivals and events all over western Europe, had never actually seen a drift net in action. He was very pleased, or should I say very surprised, when the first silver herring appeared hanging in the net. We only caught 21 herring that day. If we had been doing this for a living we would have starved, but we just wanted the thrill of catching a few fish to justify the trip.

Going on, we motored into a low autumn sun. A breeze had got up and the cold spray was hitting our faces. We envied the Felixstowe Ferry fishermen standing in their warm wheelhouse as they pounded past us, returning to the Deben bar. Once in the river we cut the engine, pulled up the forelug and mizzen and enjoyed a cracking sail up the river. Pearl and Mike gutted the fish and in the evening we ate them and discussed fish recipes and the art of smoking fish.

Before refrigeration, fish could only be kept by salting them, soaking the fish in a mixture of brine (salt and water). However to make salted fish more palatable and full of flavour they were hung up over a fire and smoked. Red herring treated in this way could be kept for about a year. When Mike smoked herring he used the English cold smoke method, soaking the herring briefly in salt and then hanging them over a fire of oak sawdust for 12-16 hours.

The East Anglian Home Fishery started about October 10 and the Scottish boats came down and worked, mainly from Yarmouth. The Lowestoft boats were mostly locally owned and crewed by men from the villages and beach landings along the coast. These were quite separate communities from the trawlermen who lived near Lowestoft and worked all the year around. In the nineteenth century the Scottish fish lassies came south by train to pack the salted herring into barrels, but in the final years after World War II it was mostly Irish women who came over for the herring season. Many smokehouse owners followed the fleet around, having smokehouses in the different ports on the East Coast and in the West Country.

There were hundreds of smokehouses in Lowestoft and Great Yarmouth, although many of these were just backyard operations. The fish curers used to go down to the fish market, buy the catch as the boats came in, and then take the fish back for smoking. Because of over-fishing by trawlers in the North Sea there was a total ban on herring between 1977 and 1980, which allowed the species to recover. But the herring is still in short supply and the remaining smoke houses at Lowestoft, Yarmouth and Whitby used herring from Scotland, Norway or even Iceland

The herring destined to become kippers at Lowestoft are gutted and slit open and then soaked in salt brine for fifteen minutes. Until about 1980 herring were salted far longer, but the modern palate does not like a kipper to taste too strongly of salt. The herring were packed on 'balks'; light poles, and strung across the smokehouse. Bloaters are simply whole, un-gutted herring that have been fastened to a 'speek', a light wooden pole, and smoked. Sprats are also smoked regularly but most types of fish can be smoked. Some larger fish, such as salmon, take two nights before they are ready to eat. This process is a simple, but effective way of turning ordinary fish into a delicacy.

I was told in 2000 that there were two smokehouses left in Great Yarmouth; one was being turned into an art gallery, but the other was reported to be still smoking fish for export. In Lowestoft three smokehouses were in operation and Will Buckenham's Old Smoke House in Ragland Street was by far the oldest. In fact it is a listed building, built in 1760 as the stables for the Vicarage and was later turned into two smokehouses. The Old Smoke House stands in an area of tightly packed Victorian terraced houses and because of complaints, the smoking can only take place at night. A pile of sawdust, mostly oak, is lit on the floor and as the smoke rises up it cures the herring and then escapes through an opening in the roof. The sides of the smokehouse are black with dried salts and soot.

There were also smokehouses in most of the longshore fishing villages. The one at Kessingland remains intact but is used as a store for the Post Office. In Southwold, sprats were smoked, and herring for bloaters, both of which were sold in the town. In the 1930s Sid Dunton of East Street had the largest Southwold smokehouse that could take a 'Last' (10,000 herring) but smoking was gradually reduced to a few backyard operations. The

Alan filling the Old Smoke House, Lowestoft with herrings for overnight smoking.

small smokehouse on the Fishermen's Flats at Walberswick was destroyed in the 1953 Floods, but a new one was built to replace it. This holds about 2000 herring and ferryman David Church uses it to smoke herrings he has caught.

At Orford, Frank Berrett ran a smokehouse in Baker's Lane until 1939. Richard Pinney, one of the early escapees from the London rat-race, came to Gedgrave (Ged'gov), a hamlet near Orford, and amongst his other entrepreneurial activities, he started a smoke-house. Prior to this smoked fish had been a cheap diet for working families, but Richard Pinney promoted them as a delicacy for the wealthy newcomers to the area. Orford became so well known for smoked food that Steve Richardson reopened his grandfather Berrett's small smokehouse in Baker's Lane.

Chapter Seven

TRIPS FROM THE ORWELL

The natural River Orwell dried out at the top end in the same way as the Deben, Stour and Blackwater still do. Ships bound up-river would anchor in the deep water of Butterman's Bay off Pin Mill and wait for the flood tide to take them up to the quays of Ipswich. When outward bound, Pin Mill was a good place to come ashore to fill-up the freshwater barrels in the stream beside The Hard, have pint in the 'Butt and Oyster' and take the ebb tide down to Harwich. Most of the people living at Pin Mill got their livelihoods from working on the water, so when the hamlet wanted to commemorate Queen Victoria's Jubilee in 1898 they raised enough money to bring shingle up river and create the Jubilee Hard.

On a wet afternoon in May 1971 we trudged down Pin Mill Hard to join the *Convoy* on a trip to Kent. The tide was ebbing, exposing the mud at the bottom of the hard and we had to push the barge's boat through this grey ooze. Once afloat, Richard Duke ran us out in his barge's boat to the *Convoy,* lying on the buoys below Butterman's Bay.

Richard was a kind of one-man barge revival movement. He had hoped to go to sea in square riggers, but the last British 4-masted barque *Garthpool* was lost in 1928 just as he left school. Richard became a tanker captain in the Merchant Navy and then went ashore, but was drawn back to sea. It became his life's mission to restore sailing barges and enjoy himself while he did it.

Richard and Annie Duke brought a series of sailing barges back to life and the 88ft (26.82m) *Convoy* was the largest of these. Going down into the hold she was like a floating barn which had been simply converted for living aboard. They had already sold the barge *Millie* and Richard, Annie and their family were living aboard the barge *Leslie West* near the 'Butt & Oyster' when in 1968 the *Convoy* was condemned after being squeezed in Tilbury Dock.

Richard, always a man to spot a bargain when he saw one, was off at once and bought the crippled barge. The boxy mulie barge *Convoy* had been built in 1900 to carry 10-ton blocks of stone from Portland to Dover for the construction of Dover Harbour breakwater. She was very strong, but when she became a motor barge iron girders were placed across the hold to strengthen her further. When they got *Convoy* back to Pin Mill the bent iron girders were taken out and the oak hull went back into shape. Richard had saved a barge and obtained a good hull cheaply.

The morning after we boarded, the *Convoy's* two diesels sprung into life and we headed off down through Harwich Harbour and out to a calm sea. Ahead 'under way' off Walton Naze, we could see two sailing barges, *Millie* and *Venture*. They looked magnificent, black hulls and a towering mass of brown canvas, but with little wind they were hardly moving. The *Millie* had a small engine, but *Venture* was still a pure sailorman, just as she had been when she came out of trade eight years earlier. As we caught up with them, one of the crew of the *Venture* stood on the bow ready to throw a towline. The *Convoy* took her in tow (fee. gallon of vino, although I have no doubt Richard would have done it for nothing) and we hurried on towards the Spitway, a channel over the sandbanks which form a barrier off the Essex coast.

After six hours we were at Southend with the other barges, waiting to race the next day. However Richard decided he did not want to spend the night rolling about off Southend at anchor and headed off towards Queenborough, across the Thames Estuary near the mouth of the River Medway.

Richard, standing in his wheelhouse in his duffel coat and Merchant Navy cap worn at a jaunty angle, looked every inch what he was, a World War II tanker captain. Although he loved and understood barges, he handled the *Convoy* as if she was a big ship. No dashing about the estuary, we waited until the main shipping channel was clear and then, powered by the throbbing Gardners crossed over to the mouth of the Medway.

In the Southend Barge Match the next day the first barge home was *Centaur*, which proudly flew the Duke house flag. She was another of Richard's rescue jobs. I had first seen the *Centaur*, one of the fine wooden barges built by Canns at Harwich, in 1954, when she was discharging in Felixstowe Dock. There was hardly any paint on the deck and a lot of frayed rope in the rigging. Her skipper had been treated with guarded respect as he was a 'teddy boy' and thought to be a very hard man. After her trading had finished the barge had been cut down to a timber lighter at Heybridge, when Richard bought her and with secondhand gear he had got her back sailing again.

Richard had instigated *Centaur's* return to sail in 1966 and the next time I saw her was off Clacton Pier under full sail, and with a fair wind and brightly painted hull she looked fifty years younger. She was doing passenger charter work from Maldon at the time but I

The spritty barge *Centaur* sailing into Ipswich Dock in 1987. On the right is the new Whisstock-built schooner *Red Jacket,* which had come round to Ipswich to be fitted out.

Gwen Buckenham outside the Old Smoke House, Lowestoft with split herring on a balk ready to be cold smoked into kippers.

The small spritty barge *Cygnet*, built in 1881, worked within Harwich Harbour taking wheat from farm wharves on the River Stour to mills, seen here at Snape Maltings, 2000.

The 18ft (6.7m) Suffolk beach boat *Three Sisters*, a boat for all seasons.

The Ferry Dock on the day of the Woodbridge Boat Sale, spring 1961. The Faversham staysail barge *Pretoria* was built in 1902 and carried cargoes under sail until 1954 when Cdr. Horncastle converted her for living aboard and cruising. The barge was sold in 1963 to become a café, but all that remains of her now is the bottom, in the mud at Maldon.

The Woodbridge boatyard owner Frank Knights on the Ferry Quay with beach boat *Pet* in 1992. Frank trained at Robertson's yard and in 1940 set out with George Arnott for the Dunkirk Evacuation in *L'Atalanta*. After spending the war years in the Royal Navy Frank returned to open Frank Knights (Shipwrights) on Ferry Quay in 1947.

The steel mulie barge *Will Everard* at the Common Quay, Ipswich after discharging a freight in 1963. Before an engine was fitted, *Will Everard* could load 280 tons to sea and was much larger than the average spritty barge. This was achieved because she has a very deep hull.

Richard Duke aboard his mulie barge *Convoy* at Pin Mill in 1971. The *Convoy* was berthed astern of the barge *Leslie West* which Richard, Annie and their family lived aboard. The *Convoy* later became a part of a pub on the Thames and sank near Wandsworth Bridge.

am not sure this earned much more than her keep. The *Centaur's* jib had split during the Southend race and was brought aboard the *Convoy* for repair. It was spread out on the saloon floor, formerly the aft end of the hold, and everyone took it in turns to use the sail-maker's palm and needle to re-sew the stitching.

After Southend we crossed over to Kent to get ready to watch the Medway Match. In the calm, hot afternoon we went across in the barge's boat to look at the barge hulks in Shepherds Creek. There were then hundreds of barges, left over from the days before World War I when over two thousand had been trading, lying in various states of decay around the Thames Estuary.

There is something very haunting about the white, weather-worn timbers of an abandoned barge. One can stand on the remains of the deck (if there is one) and dream of how it felt to run down the Swin in a full gale or to drift up under the London Bridge with the mast lowered on the deck. Some of the barges there were very old, and some people believe that the little swim-head barge *Admiral Blake* dates from the 1790s. The *Ernest Piper* only dated from 1898, but her twisted hull had filled with water and it was obvious she would never sail again so we cut out her name board. Then Colin Fox and I tossed a coin to see who should have it. I lost.

Apart from having a good sail, turning to windward up to Gillingham with the new re-juvenated staysail, the day following the Medway Match passed without incident. Early on Tuesday morning we set off for Pin Mill, towing the *Venture*, but the fog kept coming down so we had to anchor twice and wait for it to clear. The trip across was peaceful and when the wind got up we cast off the *Venture* who arrived back at Pin Mill later that evening.

The *Reminder* and other spritty barges on The Hard at Pin Mill after the 1984 Pin Mill Barge Match.

When we reached Pin Mill the tide was not high enough to get the barge back to her berth on the Hard. Richard headed at speed for the 'barge channel', a passage across the ooze inshore of the yacht moorings. When the huge wooden barge hit the soft mud her flat-bottom allowed her to skate over the mud until she was several inches out of the water above her waterline. But she still did not reach her berth. The dolly line, a wire rope with its own wind-lass, was run out to a post on the Hard and the 88ft (26.82m) flat-bottomed barge was dragged over the mud until the hull was nine inches out of the water and she could be safely berthed.

A fortnight later we went off to Kent again. This time to help publicise the opening of the new Dolphin Barge Yard Museum at Sittingbourne. Richard stood at the wheel and Annie did the cooking for the large, cheerful party. It was cold, but there was little need for pilotage because the visibility was very clear. The low land of Essex was little more than a faint line on the horizon after the Spitway, but the Downs of Kent showed up clear-ly from the West Swin. Here the sheets were eased and with the stiff easterly breeze little clouds of spray came over the bows, as she bashed against the flood tide past the Isle of Sheppey. It was more sheltered under Warden Point and then the sails were stowed as we came up the West Swale to anchor off Milton Creek, which leads up to Sittingbourne. Richard and Joe went off in the boat to pick up Les William, a retired barge skipper who was going to pilot us up the narrow creek. All went well to start with, then on a tight bend after Adelaide Dock, a silted up cement barge dock, the barge went hard aground at the stern and the props churned up black mud. The barge dragged herself off, only to catch the mud on the other shore. Les chose this moment to reveal that he had not been up Milton Creek for over twenty years. Nobody said a word.

When we reached the Crown Quay, Sittingbourne we had to wait for a little coaster to leave. Unfortunately the flood tide 'took charge' of the barge and she wedged herself across the creek with the bows firmly ashore on the far bank. As the ebb started everyone worked like mad to get her off before the falling tide left her stranded. The more speed, the greater the confusion and I suppose Joe falling off the bow marked the highest point of our problems. He departed spreadeagled into some of the most polluted waters in Britain, thanks to the paperworks. Locals wanted to rush Joe off to hospital to have his stomach pumped, but he was made of tougher stuff. Apart from his long (if highly fashionable) hair curling more vigorously, he suffered no ill effects.

Forward, half a dozen strong men put all their strength into the windlass and hauled the *Convoy's* bow off, while the huge props dug holes in the mud aft. This sent clouds of black water down the creek on the ebb. Suddenly the barge came free and floated forwards and in seconds she was made fast alongside the Crown Quay.

At the opening of the Dolphin Barge Museum, Frank Carr made a rousing speech. The yard had been used to build and repair the sailing barges of the Dolphin Cement Works, but after the works closed few people had any use for the derelict properties along the creek. Most of the barge yards were pulled down, a few were still in use, but the Dolphin remained just the same as when the barges had left forty years earlier.

The homeward bound trip was done in fine style with a fair wind, under mains'l, tops'l and stays'l and the old barge fairly ploughed across the Thames Estuary, pushing up a great bow wave. However, we arrived at the Spitway two hours after low water, where there was the equivalent of a maritime traffic jam. Five steel ballast barges, loaded from the River Colne pits and bound for the wharves in London, were chugging around waiting for enough water. Two wooden motor barges, *Cabby* and *Hydrogen*, both ex-sailormen and deeply loaded, were also waiting. The steel ballastmen started to nose their way into the

Spitway, looking for the deep water. The *Merger* was in front but she caught the edge of the channel and all at once the others used her as a marker and steamed through. On the *Convoy* the lead line said there was a fathom and half in the channel.

After the evening meal we relaxed on the hatch tops with the brown sails straining above us as the sun set over Clacton. Five hours after leaving Crown Quay we were up to Walton Pier and life seemed very nearly perfect, but in a few minutes this suddenly changed. The tide turned against us and as so often happens, a change in the tide means a different weather pattern. As we fought the young flood a fresh NE blotted out the lights of the shipping in Harwich Harbour. In the dark we floundered around the deck stowing up the sails, it was just motoring now, as the master mariner at the wheel wanted to get into the Orwell as quickly as possible.

There were two coasters astern and Richard asked us to watch out for ships coming down from Ipswich. We could see little from the bow in the driving rain until we spotted the mud off Collimer Point, but we had run ashore before the news reached the wheelhouse. However we were out of the way of all the shipping and in a safe place to spend the night. Next morning, before dawn, and still in the pouring rain, the last four miles were completed to Pin Mill and *Convoy* was returned to her berth on Pin Mill Hard with the other barges.

Of all the East Coast estuaries, the River Orwell has been changed the most by the hand of man, yet it is still one of the most beautiful. We became aware of this during a day's barge trip we had in 1980, on Paul's sailing barge *Ena*. Going down river from the Dock

The start of a Pin Mill Barge Match in 1965. Left to right: *Memory, Venture, Millie, Ardeer, May* and *Mirosa.* The *Kitty, Westmoreland* and eventual winner, skippered by 73-year-old Jack Spitty, *Edith May* are behind the barge's sails. In 2000 only *May, Mirosa* and *Kitty* were still sailing.

The races for trading barges ended in 1963 and the early revival races followed the old practices, limiting the size of the crews. Once in a Medway Match the *Edith May* was disqualified from winning for having too many crew. In his defence Jack Spitty said 'Would it help you to know we are all over seventy.'

On the left, a new yacht is ready to be launched at Whisstock's yard, Woodbridge with the huge motor cruiser *Gitala* taking shape on the quay, 1987. Since 1975 the mulie barge *Thalatta* has come up to Woodbridge every year for the Town Regatta.

End yard, Cliff Quay and the Power Station were quickly passed, then all at once either shore opened out into glorious farm and parkland, coming right down to the water's edge. This is not a natural landscape, but one largely created by the gentry, whose object was to surround their grand houses with a tranquil vista, but they actually created a truly lovely river for later generations.

Once out of the Orwell, the salty old town of Harwich sits perched on the end of a peninsula. An old sailor once told me that Harwich was full of churches and pubs, the two ways that sailors consoled themselves for the difficulties of harsh lives at sea. Harwich really got put on the map in 1674 when Charles II authorised the construction of a Royal Dockyard right on the tip of the peninsula.

The Naval Dockyard vanished under a new roll-on, roll-off ferry terminal in 1964, but several hundred men-of-war, and then large merchant sailing ships were built there. The builders were W.B. McLearon until 1927 when their business closed down. It was McLearon who built the barges *Thalatta* and *Ena* at the same time in 1906, but could not find buyers for them. These barges lay ready for launching until the wood turned black and eventually Groom bought the *Thalatta* and the *Ena* was sold to Paul's. For the next seventy-two years *Ena* took grain from the London docks to R. & W. Paul's mills and the maltings at the end of Ipswich Dock, first as a mulie sailing barge and then as a motor barge. Her owners converted her back to a sailing barge, and she was the last of the Ipswich barge fleet until she was sold in 2000.

On the day we sailed on *Ena* there was little wind and the heavy sails hung down limply, while the wash from passing craft made the wheel kick. We returned under power, passing the peaceful green parkland of the long forgotten genteel families and suddenly, on reaching the power station on the Ipswich shore the whole character of the river changed. The river surface had a blue-red stain of oil. Perhaps this oil had been quietly pumped from one of the silent ships at Cliff Quay. In those days no one had explained to ship's engineers about the dangers of such actions to the environment. More likely the penalties of such actions had not yet deterred ships from using the river as a dumping ground.

The *Ena* slid back into her berth at the Dock End yard beside the lock gates. The barge yard had not been altered much from the Edwardian era when Paul's had their barges built here. At that time the Port of Ipswich above the lock gates was more or less as the nineteenth century had left it. Victorian mills, maltings and warehouses had replaced most of the Tudor port and only the concrete silos acknowledged the twentieth century.

Ipswich has always been a curious mixture of an ancient past and a progressive future. It was the first place on the East Coast to hold a festival of the sea when Maritime Ipswich was held in 1982. At that time some councillors considered the dock to be redundant and thought it should be filled in to make a lorry park. Maritime Ipswich was the concerted effort of many local people to try and point out that the dock was an asset to the town.

The barge *Cabby* has never changed hands, but as the company that had her built has been divided up, she now sails under the new house flag of Hays. Built in 1928, the *Cabby* was the last wooden barge to be built, and finished up working as a motor barge. She was then returned to sail as a company promotion barge. Pearl and I boarded *Cabby* at

On the barge *Cabby* as she passes the cruise liner *Spendour of the Sea* at Parkeston Quay, 2000. On the left is mate Christine Swift, then at the wheel actor Bernard Hill, who played the part of the captain in the film *Titanic*, and skipper Gerard Swift.

Woolverstone Marina in 2000 and voyaged down the River Orwell, still lined with fine oaks and green parkland. Decades before, there had only been yachts tugging at moorings at Bourne Creek and Pin Mill but in more recent years forests of masts have marked marinas at Ipswich, Bourne Creek, Woolverstone, Levington and just around Bloody Point in the Stour at Shotley. Pin Mill is no longer the main yachting centre of the river, as Arthur Ransome and many others of the old-time muddy boot yachtsmen had known it. The new generation of urban, boating people expect to step aboard their craft in low shoes, from a pontoon.

In *Cabby*, we sailed up the River Stour, which unlike the Orwell has changed very little. This is a straight estuary, with no bends to break the force of the wind, such as Collier Point on the Orwell or Prettyman's Point on the Deben. The Stour can be very exposed and with the wind blowing all the way from Harwich an incredible sea builds up at high water and thunders against Mistley Quay. Manningtree, just around the corner, does have a little shelter, but is shallow and the tide only floods the ooze flats for a short period every day. This does not deter a hardy band, clad in their wellington boots, from making Manningtree their home anchorage.

Mistley used to be famous for its swans, the second largest colony in Britain. They fed on the waste coming out of the mills and maltings and although most of the mills have closed many beautiful swans remain, living on the waste of industry. They do not seem bothered by the noisy boating activities that worry wildlife on many rivers.

L'Atalanta and the *Pet* at Albion Wharf with Paul's Home Warehouse in the background at Ipswich Dock during Maritime Ipswich, 1982.

Chapter Eight

THE OYSTER CREEKS

Compared to the River Deben entrance, which is a narrow dangerous channel between shingle knolls, the entrance to the River Blackwater and Colne appears to be a wide expanse of open sea. It is nearly four miles across where the two rivers flow out into the bottom of the Wallet channel. The first time I sailed past the Colne Bar buoy I found it hard to believe that there could even be a river there.

This was in 1952, and we were bound for West Mersea over a glassy calm sea. Ahead, in our path, was a transom-sterned smack trawling on the port tack. The smack's topsides were black and rough with countless coats of tar and her sails were old, faded and heavily patched. Two elderly men on the smack waved us over and asked us what the time was. I think they were probably Alf and Cliff Claydon on the Maldon based *Joseph T*, but by the look of these ancient smackmen, and their timeworn craft, they should have asked us which century they were in.

I was surprised, even then, that there were still craft fishing under sail. When I suggested this to our skipper Arthur Hunt, who as a young man in about 1910 had skippered the Bradwell stackie barge *Dover Castle,* he laughed and said 'there's always smacks fishing here'.

In fact, we were witnessing the end of working sail on the East Coast. When we entered West Mersea, a labyrinth of creeks behind Mersea Island at the entrance of the Blackwater, there were more smacks, but all motorized, lying on moorings just past the Packing Shed Island. I went off and rowed under their sterns so that I could read the names: *Gracie, Our Boys, Pilgrim* and many more I have forgotten. These elegant workboats were built in the Victorian and Edwardian eras to dredge oysters and catch sprats in the narrow channels and creeks along the Essex coast. To do this they had to be very good at beating against the wind, up narrow channels. The Essex smacks, which were mostly built in yards on the River Colne, were very similar to the Victorian racing yachts. This was not surprising since Aldous, Harris Bros, and Stones, all played a part in developing the Victorian yachts, and many smackmen spent their summers as paid hands on yachts and returned home for fishing in the winter.

In the autumn, when the smackmen returned home from a summer of big yacht racing, village regattas were arranged and the smack races were major events. Sometimes, if a fisherman was having a good summer earning high prize money for the owners, who took the cups and the glory, he would write back to a yard and order a new smack. The instructions included details such as 'make her like the *Daisybell*, but a bit longer and finer'. Aldous also built hulls 'on spec' and sold them either as yachts or as smacks. Howard, at Maldon, did the same and in 1881 he built a new yacht hull. But a yacht skipper bought this hull and changed her into the 50ft (15.24m) smack *Sunbeam*. When he was home in the winter he used her for fishing. In Essex the fishermen liked to have fast smacks so that they could get home quicker and if they won the smack class in one of the regattas they became local heroes.

The great recorder of Essex's maritime past was Hervey Benham, whose books, starting with *The Last Stronghold of Sail* in 1948, lit the touch paper to the whole era of restoring traditional sailing craft that has continued in Essex ever since. Hervey lived at 'Mersea City', the quiet end of West Mersea, in a flat-roofed house with a beautiful view across the creek and the marshes beyond. He was a realist, he did after all successfully manage the family newspaper business, but at the same time he was a romantic who loved the past. His role as editor of the *Essex County Standard* meant he was expected to influence events, but at the same time to stay in the background. In private he was a great storyteller, with a wide range of tales told in dialect. Many of these went into his books, he understood the golden age of sail in Essex and was able to portray it in a very readable manner.

When Hervey Benham first went down to West Mersea, in the 1930s, the men who had known the golden era of sail between about 1880 and 1914 were still there and were very happy to talk about it. They remembered the years when some 1300 smacks and barges were registered on the Rivers Colne and Blackwater alone and when some 1500 men and boys worked in the Essex oyster industry. This massive fleet was made up of small wooden sailing craft and there was not a single steam tug, only one steam dredger.

Some of the barge owners, such as Clem Parker of Bradwell, had fleets of sailing barges in the stackie trade, but most of the craft were fishing vessels owned by the men who sailed

The staysail barge *Mirosa* and the stowboater (sprat fishing smack) *ADC* running back to win their classes in the 1974 Colne Race. The *Mirosa* is really the perfect barge and has had a very successful racing career. Built at Maldon in 1892 by John Howard and owned and very well maintained by Peter Dodds since 1977, she was the only barge still sailing without an engine in 2000.

The wooden spritty barge *Gladys* chasing the *Cabby* in the 2000 Pin Mill Barge Match.

The Harwich built bawley *Helen & Violet* in the Colne Race, 1982. When this sailing shrimper was built in 1906 she was at the cutting edge of inshore fishing technology, but these beautiful craft have such a strong fascination on the minds and imagination of some coastal seafarers that they have been saved from destruction and preserved.

The Blackwater smack *Boadicea* rounding the Wallet-Spitway buoy in the East Coast Old Gaffers Race, 1998. The *Boadicea* was built at Maldon in 1808 and since about 1938 has been owned by three generations of the Frost family.

Ian Smith's bawley *Bona* in the 1998 East Coast Old Gaffers Race. When the EC Old Gaffers Race was begun in 1963 it was started off Osea Island. Later, following a collision between the *Pembeth* and the *Fanny,* it moved to Stone Point in 1967 and remained there until 1997 when it moved to West Mersea.

them. Brightlingsea had by far the largest fleet of smacks, in fact far larger than the home waters were able to support. In order to find a living, the Brightlingsea men went wherever there were oysters and most fishermen in other places regarded them as poachers. Hervey Benham recorded that when he first went to Falmouth there were men who still remembered seeing Essex smacks come beating in past Pendennis Castle with the hated CK registration letters on their sails.

By the end of the eighteenth century the Brightlingsea smacks were sailing to the Channel Islands and Gorey, on Jersey, became the main base there. In the nineteenth century they were going around Land's End to dredge in Swansea Bay off the Mumbles and onwards as far north as the Solway Firth. The Essex smacks happily raided the French oyster grounds, but their hardest trade of all was dredging deep-water scallops off the Terschelling Light on the north coast of The Netherlands. These smacks were known as 'skillingers' and were often caught out, deeply loaded, in the full fury of a North Sea gale. In Brightlingsea church there are tablets to five smacks recording that twenty-seven lives were lost in the great gales of 1883-4. In a small community like Brightlingsea it meant that nearly everyone lost a relative.

Sail lasted longer in the Thames Estuary than in most places, because these craft were operating in sheltered waters, but by rights, the traditional sailing craft should have finished on the Essex coast in the 1950s. It is said that a wooden boat will last about as long as a man's life, that is anything up to about a hundred years, but long before that the hulls have grown weak. There is a saying that 'old boats, like old men, leak a lot'. The people who wanted to go on sailing traditional craft for pleasure had to rebuild them.

We sailed south, to West Mersea, every year to join in the events for these restored craft and almost got to know the passage off by heart. First, after leaving the Deben, there is a problem of getting behind the ships going into Harwich, then, past Walton Pier the course increasingly turns to the south-west. After this comes the boring ten miles between Walton and Clacton piers, then Jaywick in the distance over the shallow ground and finally, through the haze, appears Mersea Island, which seems to be holding the entrance to the Blackwater and Colne Rivers apart.

Once, in 1973, when coming down in *L'Atalanta,* the prop shaft came un-coupled as we left the Deben. 'Not a problem' I announced 'we will get the sails up'. It was heavy work for me and David and Erica Jolley. We set the gaff mainsail and then the big jib which filled the whole fore triangle. *L'Atalanta* loved it, lay over gently and smashed off down the Wallet, throwing up little clouds of spray. It was a joy to be at the wheel on a day like that, but with westerly breezes, getting into the labyrinth of creeks that make up the West Mersea anchorage was going to be the real test. We could have picked up a spare mooring in Mersea Quarters, but it is very hard work to row from there up to the town landing.

Sitting at the wheel as we sailed into Mersea Quarters, I thought that if we got the sheets in really hard *L'Atalanta* would sail as close to the wind as possible and we would be able to get up Thorn Fleet and pick up a mooring. I was cutting it fine. Thorn Fleet is a narrow creek, lined with yacht moorings and with no room to tack. Our progress, close-hauled, was swift, as we wove between yachts at great speed. Then, off the Packing Shed Island, we came correctly up into the wind as David fished up one of Doug Stoker's moorings. Two years later I tried to do the same but then it was a case of pride before a fall. The crew this time was old Bill Coke and my fourteen-year-old daughter Caroline. Again it was a good sail in about a force 4 and it seemed a pity to put the engine on and spoil it. We went bowling up the Thorn Fleet, but this time the wind was in a slightly different direction. We came head to wind just before the Packing Shed with no room to tack. The big jib flapped, we fell off the wind and gently slid up on the leeward mud. Later a helpful boatman towed us up to a mooring.

With *Crangon,* half the size, I did better and sailed right up Thorn Fleet and into the Ray Channel. Doing this on another occasion, I scrambled up on to the tiny foredeck and let the anchor go, only to see the end of the rope slip over the bow. In a sort-out on passage someone had untied it, a simple mistake, but we felt very foolish. 'I've lost the anchor!' I cried in complete despair, and added a few more words. Jonathan was very cross, 'I don't know why you're swearing, it's my anchor!' Peter Clarke, as an excuse to get out on the water, was operating a launch that day and I told him about our lost anchor. Later in the week his sons dredged it back up and I paid him £20. They are a helpful crowd at Mersea.

Over the decades the number of traditional craft sailing on the Blackwater has steadily increased and this was reflected in the number of entrants to the Old Gaffers Races. In 1979 this race on the Blackwater attracted a hundred entries for the first time and several of these were yachts and smacks which had been restored. It was not until the following year that the first bawleys, *Doris* and *Helen & Violet,* with the traditional loose-footed mainsail rig, took part.

L'Atalanta was hopeless at sailing in light airs, so when the 1979 race started with the usual early morning drift down the Blackwater with the ebb tide, most of the fleet sailed off ahead of us. On the return beat up the river to Stone Point the wind started to freshen. The smacks and bawleys were about a mile ahead but when we were off the Bradwell Flats the wind increased to about force 6 and rain showers came blowing towards us. If we had been cruising I would have reefed and changed the big headsail for a smaller jib, but I hung on and in the gusts the lee deck vanished about 18 inches below the water. We picked up places and amongst the boats we overtook was Nick Hardinge's *Doris* and then the *Helen & Violet*. We were not too surprised, because at the time it was believed that the loose-footed mainsail rig was very slow.

Two years later we came out of West Mersea with *L'Atalanta*, rounded the Nass beacon and ran up the Blackwater for the start of the Old Gaffers Race at Stone Point. We were relaxing and chatting over a cup of tea, when someone remarked 'what's that?' and I turned from the wheel to look astern. A bawley with a cloud of sail was approaching at speed. As she passed us we could hear the noise of water around her bow and aft, sitting calmly at her long tiller, was Jim Lawrence. The pillar of canvas above him was his own creation.

That year the Old Gaffers Race was a flop for us, the wind dropped, we retired and motored back to join the fleet at anchor off Stone Point. However *Helen & Violet,* with her new sail plan, won the prize for the first ex-fishing boat which was the beginning of a long series of racing successes.

The first Old Gaffers Race on the East Coast was sailed in 1963 and its success was due to the fact that only gaff-rigged craft, mostly dating from before the golden age just before World War I, took part. In the early days taking part was more important than winning, but a number of boats have dominated the prize list. First it was David Cook, with the little 1872 Itchen Ferry *Fanny,* and then Dick Harman with his 1890 smack *ADC,* Gayle Heard was almost unbeatable with his 1910 day racer *Jade* and then became even more unbeatable with the 1908 prawner *Laura*.

By the 1990s the supply of old work boats suitable for restoration was running out, but the demand for them was still there. Johnnie Milgate, the Peldon shipwright and successful racing skipper of the smack *Peace*, took this thirst for the past further. In 1998 he led a party which dug the rotten hulk of the 44ft 1884 smack *ABC* out of the mud at West Mersea, where she had lain peacefully and forgotten for about fifty years.

On a mild winter's day in 1998 I walked along the top of the Strood Channel river wall at the top end of Mersea's creeks, past 'Mersea City' and Benham's house, to where two launches were engaged in trying to raise the large, rotten hulk out of the mud. This was not a piece of maritime archaeology, but a venture to bring life back to one of Brightlingsea's deep- water oyster-dredging smacks.

Shipwrights Brian Kennell and Shaun White had already put air bags around the hulk that was buried in the mud. At the top of high water springs (the highest tides) two launches tried to tow the hulk free of the mud where it had rested for about sixty years. For a long time nothing happened, but at high water, the air bags moved, the hulk floated and the launches steadily moved it to a hard at the top of Mersea.

The little party of smack-savers and watchers moved off to the 'Victory' where Doug Stoker, who had been fishing from Mersea all his life, told us that just at the end of World War II the boys used to go and play on the abandoned houseboat *Pioneer*. However Doug knew nothing of her history before that. When the tide had receded we all walked back to the hard to find the beautiful counter-sterned smack *Pioneer*. Most of the timber that stuck out of the mud was rotten, but below this at about deck level she was almost intact. Even the bungs were still in the wet wells where her catch had been kept alive. When the 58ft (17.98) *Pioneer* was built in 1864, the smack owners of Brightlingsea were concentrating on dredging scallops off the Dutch Friesian islands, off Terschelling.

The *Pioneer* and most of the other smacks were cut in half and lengthened and the

The hulk of the Brightlingsea skillinger smack *Pioneer* being floated out of the mud in the Strood channel, West Mersea in 1998.

Pioneer became a 70ft (21.34m) ketch in 1889. In letters from Douglas French, then living in retirement in Scotland, I heard about her final days under sail. His father, Arthur French, had been the last skipper of *Pioneer*. This was in the late 1920s when the Brightlingsea Water Bailiff, Tom Poole, started buying up the old 'skillingers' and tried to keep the trade going.

Douglas French remembers going into Poole's gear store with his father and hearing Tom Poole ask him to take the *Pioneer* on another trip. Arthur French said he would not go deep sea dredging again without an engine and in about 1928 Poole put one into the smack. But she did not make many more trips, Hervey Benham recorded that the Brightlingsea *Fiona* made one of the last scalloping voyages in 1931. *Pioneer* was then sold to become a houseboat, while most of the skillingers were left to rot on the mud up in Pyefleet.

The Sailing Smack Association has listed around a hundred smacks and bawleys from both sides of the Thames Estuary, almost all dating from before 1914, which have survived. Some are little more than hulks, just about afloat, while around thirteen have been totally rebuilt and are as good as the day they were built. All these represent countless hours of hard work and considerable expense to keep them sailing, but the *Pioneer*, when she vanished into a barn overlooking the Blackwater, was by far the most ambitious of these projects.

Shaun White standing in the hulk of the *Pioneer* with Jim Lawrence and Rupert Marks at West Mersea just after she was raised. 1998.

Chapter Nine

GHOSTING DOWN THE BLACKWATER

It was very quiet just after dawn and we all moved quietly around the *Reminder's* saloon, once her cargo hold, so as not to wake everyone. The barge was berthed at the Hythe Quay, Maldon, on a rising tide. You could feel she was still firmly on the mud. Pearl and Rosemary were in the galley making the first cup of tea of the day. Suddenly the barge gave a slight movement as she floated on the rising tide and became a living creature. On deck the only person in sight was the young mate Kevin, who was busy taking in the moor-ing rope which was fastened to *Centaur.* 'Roger', he explained, referring to the skipper, 'likes her to be ready to sail'.

Shortly afterwards Roger Beckett appeared, walking down the steep hill to the Hythe with the air of man who knew exactly what to expect during the forthcoming day's sail. It was, after all, twenty-nine years since he had got the *Reminder* back under sail and he had done these charter barge trips countless times. Launched in 1929 at Mistley, the *Reminder* was almost the last working spritsail barge built. That honour went to the barge *Blue Mermaid* that was launched the following year. These two were the last of a series of steel barges built at Mistley in the inter-war period by the astute ship owner Fred Horlock. Fred had started his career on the deck of a barge and from a quarter share in the *Pride of the Stour* had quickly built up a fleet of sailing barges and moved on to operating steam ships, many of them built at his own shipyard at Mistley.

At a time in the 1920s when many of the sailing barges owned on the Thames and Medway were abandoned because of lack of work, Fred Horlock managed to capture all the work to the Mistley mills and maltings. He became a wealthy man, much to the envy of his many relations in the little town of Mistley. He owned racehorses and was very keen that his barges should win in the annual Thames and Medway barge matches. Being a good Essex man, Fred Horlock's great ambition was that his barges should beat the Kent barges owned by Everards, who were then dominating both the racing and coastal shipping trade. Harold Horlock, a distant relation and mate on some of Fred's barges, once told me that his seven steel barges were designed by 'a man from Lowestoft, I forget his name'. In the 1928 races, Everard's barges swept the board and on the steamer following the race Fred remarked to Fred Everard, 'You will have a reminder of this next year'.

This is how the barge got her name, *Reminder,* and when she turned up at the Thames and Medway races in 1929, fresh from the yard, and never having carried a cargo, she won all her classes. All this was seven decades before we set off on a day charter trip down the River Blackwater. Since then her plates have bent and her bottom has been patched up, giving more resistance to water and probably losing her speed. Back in the 1930s she had a bowsprit and set a jib and jib topsail, in fact Fred Horlock over canvassed his barges so much for racing that they had to have their sail plans cut down for normal trading. In her time as a charter barge at Maldon, *Reminder* has just been a staysail barge. The tight economics of chartering would not pay for a bowsprit and the two extra sails.

Yacht moorings have filled the waters of most East Anglian anchorages and ports, but Maldon has been left to the barges, because it dries out at low tide. The day we sailed on

Aboard the Maldon-based *Marjorie* going down the River Blackwater in 1973. To continue to sail, any form of traditional craft must find a useful role. The extra number of people aft, chimney in the deck and life-raft on the hatch tops show that *Marjorie* was then in charter work. She finished, with *Anglia*, trading in 1960 while other Ipswichmen *May, Venture* and *Spinaway C* carried some freights under sail for about another three years.

Reminder we motored away from the Hythe Quay just before high water, with the *Pudge* some way ahead of us. The engine was cut just below Northey Island and by then in the open estuary we were feeling the full force of a fresh south-westerly breeze. The foresail was set and the mainsail eased down to the sprit. The ebb had started and in the freshening breeze both barges were going over the ground at speed. We overhauled the *Pudge* before we reached Osea Island, Fred Horlock would have liked that.

We ran down to the mouth of the River Colne and here, sheltering in the Pyefleet behind Mersea Island, we saw the mulie barge *Thalatta* and the little swimhead stumpie barge *Fertile*. This has long been a place for barges to tuck into in a stiff south-westerly breeze. An account of a gale in 1936 reported forty sailing barges 'windbound' in the Pyefleet. When the wind dropped they would have sailed off over the Spitway and down to the Thames.

On *Reminder* that June day we turned back to the Blackwater. Beating into a force 6 south-westerly with the main, topsail and foresail set, we slammed into the river waves with the occasional splash of spray coming over the windward bow. A wooden-hulled barge might have leaked if she had been driven so hard, but this 'iron pot' took it all in her stride.

The flood tide was under us, so we turned to windward briskly up past Osea and then, as the river became shallow, Roger 'brought up' to anchor just below Mill Beach to wait for the tide. At this stage we all went below and had a cheerful communal meal around the saloon table. When the tide flooded we returned to Hythe Quay. The *Reminder* has a low

RS on the spritty *Reminder* running down the River Blackwater, 1999.

powered engine and prop on the quarter so progress was just as much down to the tide as to her own machinery.

Roger Beckett's researches have revealed that the first barge built in Essex was the *Experiment* in 1791 for Samuel Horlock, an ancestor of Fred Horlock. In 1796 the *Langford* was the first built at Maldon, but by that time there were already some twenty-seven Kent and London built spritsail barges owned in the Maldon area. The flat-bottomed barges were ideal for working into the creeks, but these early spritties were only about 70ft long (21.34m) and had 4ft 6in (1.4m) sides. Just right for a horse and trumbel to come alongside and unload into, but by the 1870s they had 6ft 6in (2m) sides and were becoming sea-going craft. Taking hay and straw to London must have been some of the early freights for the little 'ditch crawling' spritties, but a special type of barge was developed for this.

The Victorian 'stackie' barges had a flat sheer and wide decks and a special rig. They loaded mangolds or swedes in the hold and then put a stack of hay or straw to the deck halfway up the mast. The mainsail and foresail had reef points so that the sails could be set above the stack. A tilt was put over the stack to keep it dry and off they went for the wharves on the London River.

The only person I have ever met who remembers the stackie barges is Bob Wells, who lives on the hill just above the Hythe Quay. He first went to sea in a stackie barge skippered by his father. He recalled that although the barge sailed with a stack of hay on the deck with only half the mainsail above it, a draught created by the stack pushed the barges along quite fast.

Because of her low hull and great beam, the *Dawn* was said, by the old Maldon barge skippers, to have been the best of the stackie barges. She used to load in front of the 'Queen's Head', a berth once used by collier brigs, that has since silted up. Normally the barge loaded 130 tons to sea, but with a stack of hay or straw piled halfway up her mast, she only loaded 20 tons. Usually she sailed from the Blackwater to Carter Patterson's wharf on the Thames. Most of the other barges in the stackie trade got into trouble at some time or another, but the *Dawn* never lost a stack over the side.

In the early golden days of barges the *Dawn* could support a crew of three, skipper, mate and third hand. One of *Dawn's* first mates, after she was built at Cooks in 1897, was 'Hobby' Keeble. He went on to be the skipper of *Dawn* for over thirty years. The barge, when the stackie trade finished in the 1920s, was sold to Francis & Gilders of Colchester who were building up a fleet of 'seeking' barges, carrying cargoes anywhere. Although the *Dawn* was one of their smaller barges, Francis & Gilders went to the expense of fitting a 44hp Kelvin engine, because the *Dawn* was small enough to get under the bridges at Colchester to reach the East Mills. Hobby left Maldon under power and the new engine was still running when he reached the London Docks. As he had never taken a barge into a dock under power, he stopped the engine and went into the locks under sail, but within a year he was in the owner's office demanding a bigger engine!

Hobby was an elderly man when the barge revival started at Maldon in the early 1960s, and he was not impressed with the new breed of barge skippers. Once he stood on the Hythe Quay greatly disapproving of the way a barge was being sailed up. When the barge came alongside he regaled the young skipper with advice. 'Y'er not sailing that barge right at all. I will tell you for why. If you go on sailing a barge like that for long, you won't have a barge's sail'.

Once, when the *Dawn* was anchored off Bradwell, Gordon Swift, who fitted her out for charter work in 1966, woke just before dawn to see a figure standing at the foot of the cabin steps. He thought at first that someone was trying to steal the radio, but later thought it might have been old 'Hobby' Keeble come back to make sure the barge was alright. Maybe this was true, because the barge had lost a mate over the side. 'Hobby' was turning the barge to windward off the Blackwater when the fores'l knocked the mate overboard. The mate was a strong swimmer and shouted 'cut the boat adrift', which 'Hobby' did, but he never saw the man or the boat again. He then ran back up the Blackwater where a tug off Osea, which had seen the barge go out, came over and asked what was wrong. They went aboard and sailed the barge back to Maldon, but 'Hobby' was in such a state he couldn't speak.

Ghosts on barges are usually helpful. The Mistley barge *Repertor* had a ghost called Old Harry, who had been killed by a crane in Ipswich Dock. When the crew were below at night they sometimes heard him on deck, paying out the anchor chain so that the barge didn't drift. The old bargemen spent most of their lives afloat and their families were people they visited at the weekend, so it is not surprising that they continued to keep an eye on their beloved craft.

The return to Maldon in a barge is often more dramatic than the departure. The river dries out at low water and when the barges return on the first of the flood tide, they

The bawley *Bona* and Noel Probyn's 49ft (14.93m) 1910 yacht *Hardy* in the 1999 Old Gaffers Race.

Roger Beckett on the lee deck of the spritty *Reminder,* beating past Bradwell in the River Blackwater, 1999.

The Essex smacks *Sunbeam, Fly* and Donald Rainbird's *Mayflower* at the start of the Pyefleet Smack and Bawley Race in 1990. In this race smacks had to dredge oysters or catch and cook shrimps. To keep alive the skills of handling a smack under sail, oyster-dredging matches have also been held from Maldon and West Mersea.

The 82ft (25m) spritty barge *Dawn* in the 1986 Colne Race. The *Dawn* was built in 1897 at Maldon as a 'stackie' barge, taking hay and straw to the Thames for London street horses. *Dawn* has very low sides and bow so that she could go up creeks to load at farm wharves.

occasionally scrape the muddy bottom on the bend, but their sheer weight keeps them moving and they usually come back into the channel. The river here has long had problems with silting. The quay in front of Taylor's old sail loft, where there is now barely enough water to float a boat at high water, was in Victorian times a deep water quay area where collier brigs, drawing 12ft (3.65m) of water, came to discharge coal.

Our trip down the Blackwater on the *Reminder* ended when the anchor was dropped and the tide swung her around and a line was thrown to Richard Titchener, *Xylonite's* skipper, to haul us alongside the other barges at the Hythe Quay. Six barges lay on the quay waiting for their next charter to take them down river. From the quay it is a very short walk to the 'Jolly Sailor' or the 'Queen's Head'. In 1949, just after an engine had been fitted in the handsome barge *Phoenician,* her skipper brought her up to Maldon with a freight and then walked to the 'Jolly Sailor' for a drink. Here he got into conversation with one of the new breed of sailing barge enthusiasts. 'What do you think of having an engine in your beautiful barge, skipper?' the enthusiast asked eagerly. 'I hate it' retorted the crusty old skipper 'everything smells of diesel, that get into the lockers and even the butter tastes of diesel. Your clothes, when you put them on first thing of a morning they reek of that diesel. Oh I hate that bloody engine.'

This was just what the enthusiast wanted to hear, 'I expect skipper you would rather have your sails back again?' 'What!' snapped the indignant skipper, taking a deep sip of the beer he had just been bought, ' I have spent a lifetime of hauling and pulling my guts out on them bloody ropes. Sweating fit to bust, hauling up sails and then hauling the buggers down again. If there is one thing I hate more than the stinking engine it's those bloody sails. I never want to have anything to do with sails again!'

The *Xylonite* sailing in the Blackwater, 1999.

Chapter Ten

THE MARSH COAST

It was in May 1957 that I first sailed to the River Crouch. It was not a very happy trip. The weather was foul for much of the time. It started off well enough when we left the Deben at 2pm and caught the first of the flood tide down the coast toward the mighty River Crouch. *Sea Fever* was slow by any-one's standards, in this case moving 5 knots over the ground, and by 8pm we had let go the anchor off the little yachting town of Burnham-on-Crouch.

It was dark when we went ashore for a drink, and under the lights of the Royal Corinthian Yacht Club I had spotted a lovely sandy beach. On stepping out of the pram dinghy on to the beach I discovered to my horror that the lights had made the ooze look like sand and I sank up to my knees in cold grey mud. Somehow this rather discoloured my view of the River Crouch!

We left next morning at 9am, headed back north and got through the shallow Ray Sand Channel before the tide fell too far. Then we had to beat against the south-westerly and flood tide to get into the River Colne. *Sea Fever* was almost flat-bottomed and although she had a centreboard we spent most of the day thrashing about very close to the Buxey Sands, trying desperately to beat far enough north to catch the flood tide to take us into the River Colne.

It was a long, cold day with spray constantly falling on the deck. *Sea Fever* seldom sailed fast enough to wet the man at the tiller. It was 5pm before we were far enough up the Colne to turn into Brightlingsea Creek. Tired and in need of a meal we let the anchor go just in the creek mouth. It was not until later that I discovered there were mooring posts, just above the landing hard, that had been put there by the Royal Navy in World War II. Next morning it was blowing Force 6 NE and raining. Under power, we crept up to the posts and it was two weeks before I got my little cutter back to the Deben.

Our second attempt to reach the Crouch was much more successful. At the end of September in 1962 Pearl and I set out in *Sea Fever* for a week's cruise on the Essex coast. This time, after leaving the Deben we called in at Brightlingsea and then slid down the Ray Sand Channel off the Dengie peninsula and into the Crouch. The land is so low-lying at Foulness (which means 'headland of the wild fowl') that it is quite difficult to see where the Maplin Sands finish and the great marsh islands start. Foulness is the largest of the five marsh islands that lie to the south of the Crouch, all enclosed by earth river walls that were originally dug by hand.

There is no doubt that the sea level has risen. There is evidence of Iron Age and Romano-British Settlements on most of the Roach islands. Also, in the Blackwater, on the Stumbles inside of Osea Island there was a Neolithic settlement and the whole area was dense woodland of alder and oak. As the sea level rose, the 'wallers', men responsible for throwing low river walls, created 'innings' which once the tide was kept off them turned into rich summer grazing marsh.

On a hilltop on the south shore of the Crouch is Canewdon, which got its name because the Danish warrior king Canute beat the English King Edmund Ironside in a battle here in

1016. Canute then ruled a great North Sea empire which extended right across England and Denmark. Because Canute was an all-powerful king, his followers, who held land along the coast, came to ask him to stop the flooding and erosion. Canute, a tough administrator, took his throne down on to the beach and ordered the tide not to come in. Naturally the tide came in all the same, but Canute had made his point and said he did not want to be bothered on this subject again. That has been the attitude of central government ever since.

Fortunately, the land-owners did not listen to this message of doom and sent out more gangs of wallers to keep the tide out. The reclaiming of the Essex marshes must have been a considerable undertaking. The wall from Bradwell to Burnham-on-Crouch enclosing Dengie Marshes alone is over twenty miles long and must have called for a massive organisation to construct. The wallers are the unsung heroes of coastal Essex, yet we know less about them than we do about the men who built the Egyptian pyramids.

From the late medieval period until about 1860, the sea level fell and more marshes were walled off from the sea. Although average sea levels still rise and fall, on average they are rising more, but whether this will continue in the long term no one knows for certain. When looking back into the past one often finds that predictions about the future were totally wrong.

On our cruise in 1962 we picked up a mooring at Burnham for the first night. Burnham is a lovely little town and its waterfront is smart and clean, but this has not always been the case in Essex. Once we went ashore on the beach at the top of Cliff Reach and found it covered in rubbish and bottles, no doubt from some wild party. Quite why people sail to out of the way beauty spots, start pulling things down to make fires and after damaging the area leave a dirty mess is a mystery to me.

From Burnham we beat up to Fambridge. Next day it was bleak and raining and we ran up river just under foresail and then, above Hullbridge where it was slightly more sheltered, we put up the mainsail. I was not sure where the river ended, it seemed to wind on and on for a long while, but suddenly we rounded a bend and found the bridge at Battlebridge across the end of the navigation. With a strong breeze astern we had to stop quickly, so I let the anchor go and dropped the sails and *Sea Fever* swung around on the tide, a trick used on the sailing barges.

As we went back with the ebb I did not dare to tack in the narrow channel, but once we got to Brandy Hole there was enough space to start sailing again and we beat down to Burnham, then into the River Roach and let the anchor go off Roach Quay. We had never been to this remote corner of south-east England before and, having been on the boat all day, we decided to go for a walk on Foulness Island. There was not a lot to see, but on our return we had a bit of a conscience when we passed huge notices telling us that it was Government Property and we should keep out.

Although we have since popped into the Burnham River, time passes very quickly and it was thirty-one years before we returned to explore the Foulness Islands. This time we joined Shirley and Tony Judd on the 30ft (9.14m) Leigh cockler *Alice & Florrie* at North Fambridge. It turned out to be the highest tide of the year and we set off, under power, down to the River Roach and then into the Foulness archipelago. The first creek we entered was Barlinghall, then down Potton Creek between Potton Island and the mainland into Havengore Creek. We had to wait our turn to go out through Havengore Bridge and over the Broomway on to the Maplin Sands. From the Rivers Crouch and Roach, Havengore is a kind of back door entrance to the Thames, but it is not much used. It is only possible to go out of Havengore Creek and across the Maplin Sands at high water and very shortly after this the ebb tide comes out of the Thames Estuary against you.

After a brief trip out of Havengore, we came back into the River Roach and eventually anchored in Paglesham Pool. Sitting on deck we spotted the tall white sails of a bawley coming down the Roach and spent a long time speculating on which one it was. It turned out to be Jim Lawrence in his bawley *Saxonia* on a 'weekend away cruise for the boys in the sail loft'. Next morning we beat down the Roach with *Saxonia* or perhaps it is more correct to say that we started together and she soon sailed off ahead. While *Saxonia* headed back for Brightlingsea we settled down for a peaceful run right up the Crouch with all the flood tide.

Above Hullbridge we ran aground for the first time. When we had come up here with *Sea Fever* we did not have this problem, because she had a centreboard. It is amazing how much difference another foot of draft makes in shallow East Coast rivers. About 1961 Pat Fisher was skipper of Sully's auxiliary barge *Oxygen* and used to take wheat from the Royal Docks in London up to the mill at Battlesbridge. They would load wheat in the Royal Docks, London and then on a high spring tide make a passage for Battlebridge, Rochford or Fingringhoe, or on a low neap tide they would go down to Great Yarmouth. Getting up to Battlebridge was not a problem because the hufflers were really good at piloting them up. In the old days of sailing barges the hufflers had put posts on all the bends and they ran ropes ashore so that as the barges came up on the tide they could control them around the tight bends.

In the *Alice & Florrie* we grounded several times, we were probably too early on the tide, but at least when we got there we had time for a drink in the pub 'The Barge' before returning to North Fambridge.

The steel 'iron pot' spritty *Repertor* in the 1986 Colne Race. The steel hulled barges can be pressed harder in a blow than the wooden hulled barges.

Chapter Eleven

DOWN THE SWIN

The sea is like fire. It can be a good friend, but a merciless enemy. To survive at sea you have to know more or less where you are and how to get to your final destination. The start of our trip to the Thames in 2000 involved different forms of navigation on board the *Crangon.* I had for many years practised the art of dead reckoning with a chart and tide tables and drawing 'cocked hats' from bearings on the chart to work out the position. The result of all this is that you should know your position at sea. Jonathan favoured electronic instrumentation, which should give you a one hundred per cent accurate position.

It was calm when we left the mooring at 5.30am dead low water. At sea the wind started to freshen and by the time we passed Walton on the Naze and entered the Wallet channel it was Force 5 and gusting more. I hung on to the tiller while Jonathan and AJ kept putting more reefs in the mainsail and there was tremendous pressure on the sheet of the tiny jib. Water slopped over the bluff bows and the coastline of Essex became fainter as we headed for the Wallet-Spitway buoy, which marks the channel over the Buxey and down into the Swin channel and the Thames mouth.

The visibility was poor as we headed off towards the Wallet-Spitway buoy. Jonathan got out his SAT NAV, but it refused to pick up any satellites and give us our position. The motion in the tiny cuddy made it impossible to do any dead reckoning there, while the rain and spray made it unfeasible to do any in the open aft area. Jonathan and 'AJ' Paul tried to get the SAT to function so that they could transfer the position to the chart. It took all my strength to hold the tiller and I thought that if I kept Clacton Pier about six miles to the east we would soon pick up the Wallet-Spitway.

Two yachts had come out of Harwich Harbour astern of us and for a time they were just white specks on the horizon. At the bottom of the Wallet they went thrashing past us, and their crews, sitting in the cockpits in red weather waterproofs, gave us a cheerful wave. I could not read their names, but they were both about 35ft long grp yachts having a fine sail in these conditions. We must have looked very archaic, bashing along in our tubby little wooden craft.

The Spitway is the major channel in the navigation of the Essex coast. The Buxey and Gunfleet form long fingers of sands jutting out from the coast just north of the River Crouch. Big ships bound for the Thames have to go well out to sea and round the Gunfleet Head, but smaller craft can go through the Spitway, a dip in the sand off the mouth of the River Colne.

The Wallet-Spitway buoy has a bell in it, and as you get near the bell's doleful toll sounds like the wake of every drowned sailor since the beginning of time. We turned into the Spitway and with the wind astern went over the ground at a brisk speed. The SAT navigator had now decided to work and it reported we were travelling at 10mph over the ground. From the Spitway to the Thames mouth the buoys are like stepping stones. Each is just within sight of the last buoy so that we could just hop from buoy to buoy. Although the wind was picking up to a respectable Force 6, we were sailing quite close to the Maplin Sands, a thin line on the horizon, but this afforded some shelter and prevented the sea from getting up, allowing us to crack along at a fine lick. In this sheltered water 'AJ' got out a flask of tea and there was a series of dull thuds from the Ministry of Defence's firing range over on Foulness Island. Our fast passage meant high morale and we joked that we were going so fast a shell would not catch up.

The coast was bending to the south all the time and as we passed each buoy we headed closer into the wind. By the time we reached the Blacktail Spit, at the bottom of the Maplins, the wind and short steep seas were dead on our bow. We could now see the high ground of the Isle of Sheppey over on the Kent shore at the mouth of the Thames. Perhaps we should have plugged on in the slight shelter of Shoeburyness on the Essex coast, but I thought we would try and get over to Kent and into the River Medway on the last of the flood. Crossing the Thames mouth in a Force 6, wind over tide, turned *Crangon* into a semi-submersible, there was water everywhere. Some waves rushed up the side of the bows and filled up the tiny foredeck, while some of the spray drove aft, stinging our faces as we stood bent against the force of the wind.

Several large cargo vessels were coming up from the east and we had to hang around on the edge of the main channel to the Thames until there was a gap to cross over to the River Medway. It is amazing how quickly sea conditions change. Quite suddenly we were under the shelter of the Kentish coast and the sea was much smoother. Through the rain the Sheerness wharves appeared, and the flood tide carried us into the calm waters of the mighty Medway.

The plan was to spend the night at Queenborough, in the Swale behind Sheppey, and then take the next day's flood up the Thames. No one bothered us as we picked up the visitors' mooring buoy at Queenborough eight hours after leaving our Deben mooring. Most of our sleeping bags and food had been stored in bin liners so they were dry, but everything else in the cuddy was soaked. We tied our wet belongings up in the rigging to dry, then lay on the floor under the shelter of the engine box, which we hoped would afford shelter from the wind, while we ate some food. It was all very uncomfortable and wet and we looked longingly at the pub at the top of landing hard.

We cheered up when we headed for the shore and morale lifted as we entered the warmth of the pub, but Jonathan and AJ thought there might be somewhere more exciting in the little town. We set out on foot to explore the delights of Queenborough. Jonathan and I were rather taken with a fine old gaff cutter, the *Prince of Wales*, which was hauled ashore near the creek. She had been built as one of the police boats, which had once patrolled under sail in the River Colne to prevent smacks from poaching oysters from the Colchester fishery.

I remembered an old Essex fisherman telling me once about the Colne fishery police cutters. How the policemen were always told that when they ran alongside a smack to inspect her for illegal oysters, they were never to put their hands on the rails because the smackmen, who wore hob-nail boots, would step on them and sail on. He also told me that the fishermen of Wivenhoe used to put a candle on the deck and if it blew out there was too much wind to go sea. But then he was a West Mersea man and you could hardly expect him to have much sympathy for 'foreigners' from another river.

My young companions were a bit put out that Queenborough did not have a Chinese restaurant, surely the only town in Britain which doesn't have one. They quickly solved the problem by summoning a taxi to take us on to Sheerness, the modest capital of Sheppey. In the warmth we had a long slow meal and 'AJ' told us tales of his years driving holiday trucks across Africa and the difficulties of crossing a continent without a proper road system.

We talked over the day's events and were pleased to have made a passage down the coast in difficult conditions. I suggested we had come down from Suffolk because our craft had a powerful engine. If we had relied on sail only, as the barges used to, we would have had to have gone into the Colne and waited for a more favourable 'slant' of wind to get down to the Thames mouth. AJ was interested in the Ipswich grain barges as his family, the Pauls, had owned one of the fleets. I started telling tales about sailing barges, pointing out that the spritsail rig was so handy that a sailing barge could be sailed by an old man, a boy and a dog, but it had to be a good dog.

It was still bleak when we returned to *Crangon,* but we were happy and well fed. Jonathan and I slept, heads touching, in the tiny cuddy, while AJ slept under the boom in his African tent lying on a faded Arab rug.

The bawley *Marigold* and smack *Lizzie Annie* dredging oysters on the common ground off West Mersea, 1995. This was the first of the Mersea Dredging Matches, known after its organizer as 'Charlie Harker's do', in which smacks had to try and dredge up as many oysters as possible under sail in a set time.

Chapter Twelve

HOME OF THE BARGES

The two of us sat on the hatches surveying the Lower Pool of London without comment. It was November 1956 and our sailing barge, the steel spritty *Xylonite,* had loaded about 120 tons of cattle feed at Bellamy's Wharf, Rotherhithe, for delivery to Mistley, a small town about a hundred miles away up the Essex coast. The oily tidal water washed angrily against the grimy warehouses and driftwood piled up in backwaters created by the barges moored along the wharves.

We were waiting for the tide to turn in our favour. The skipper, a young man of few words, got up and peered at the water to see if the ebb had started. Some of the driftwood began to move down the side of the barge as the mighty Thames started to flow back into the Thames Estuary some thirty miles away. The skipper said it was time to go and suggested I lower the cross-trees and then set the topsail to catch the faint breeze that was coming off the tops of the riverside buildings. As I hauled away on the halliard to set the sail some tough young seaman on the *St John,* the steamer we had loaded from, leant on the rail above and jeered at our antiquated craft. They had a point. What on earth was such a craft doing in the busy commercial world when Britain was adapting to the new age of technology?

We cast off and slowly moved away from the high sides of the steamer and her seamen with their teddy-boy haircuts set in Brilcreme and their uncharitable views of our sailing barge. Once on the tideway we were free, but there was little wind and the tide seemed set to sweep us into the lighter roads near the low warehouses and industrial buildings on the Isle of Dogs. The skipper shouted 'get ready to let the anchor go', but as I went forward, a tug, which was coming down river, came alongside and offered us a tow. I have no doubt that the skipper gave the tug master a small tip for this timely assistance, but in the quick chat they had, it turned out that the tug skipper had started in 'sailormen', a London River term for the spritsail barge, and had sympathy with our plight. That was how it was, some people wanted to get rid of the last of the long out-dated 'sailormen' and others wanted to see them go on sailing.

If my memory is correct, it took two weeks, thanks to bad weather, for us to reach Mistley and the following trip took three days. This totally unpredictable way of delivering freight seemed to be accepted, after all, barges had been sailing from the Pool of London for about a hundred and fifty years. Sometimes the owners got fed up with the delays. Once a sailing barge had taken six weeks to get from Great Yarmouth to London and when she arrived the skipper wired the owners 'Arrived Safely'. The owners wired back 'Hooray'.

It was forty-four years since we had sailed from the Thames in the deeply loaded *Xylonite*, with water sloshing along the lee deck. I thought back to those far off days as we approached the Sea Reach of the Thames in *Crangon,* having left Queenborough just after dawn. Over the decades I had been up the London River several times, but in a 22ft (6.70m) shrimper the river seemed to be a lot larger than it had been from the barge's deck.

There had been no wind in the Sea Reach, but as we reached the Lower Hope there was a faint south-westerly breeze. Off Gravesend the wind freshened and Jonathan was keen to sail the rest of the way to St Katharine's Dock near Tower Bridge, but I suggested that it was a long way and if he wanted to get there on that tide we would have to keep the engine running.

By the time we reached Grays it was a force 7 ahead and coming around Broadness into St Clement's Reach we motored into the steep brown waves in an angry head sea. The waves were so short that the bows threw up a continuous cloud of spray. It was wetter here than it had been in the open sea the day before. We hung around on the edge of the channel, bobbing up and down like a cork, as two huge ships slipped past. We had put our oilskins on off Gravesend. The great trick with oilskins is to put them on before you get wet. It is very important to keep dry on a boat because, once wet, the cold slowly takes away your strength. The truth is, I hate the water and go to any lengths to avoid getting soaked.

The old sailors used to call St Clements Fiddler's Reach, because the sailing ships tacked forwards and backwards like a fiddler playing a lively tune. What it must have been like tacking a huge three-masted East Indiaman up this Reach I cannot think, but they did it. The Pool of London is about thirty miles from the open sea so it was not an easy passage for a square rigger. The nineteenth century collier brigs used to do a 'Gravesend nip' in the Thames. They would aback their square sails and put in a board stern first across the river, which was quicker than trying to tack.

It was the tide that made it possible for sailing ships to get up the Thames. All that water comes in from the North Sea between the North Foreland and Orfordness and as the whole estuary gets narrower the water flow speeds up and increases the amount of rise and fall. At Yarmouth the tide only rises and falls a few feet, but here in the London River there is a massive rise and fall. Basically the tide runs so strongly in the Thames that it sweeps you up river whether you wish to go or not.

When we entered the Long Reach dead into the wind it was incredibly wet. We ploughed into a brown river of very angry little waves which hit the *Crangon's* bluff bows and sent up a continuous spray. But thanks to the tide we were heading up river fast. The new Port of London is mostly below the Dartford Crossing. It actually handles more tonnage than the old Port of London, but it does not have quite the grimy mystique.

The old Port of London used to start at Galleon's Reach, where the lock gates for the Royal Group of Docks allowed shipping out on to the Thames. This Reach was empty and quiet when we got there. So many buildings had been pulled down and the foreshore silted up that it was quite difficult to pick out where the Royal Group lock gates had been. The only signs of activity were the cranes whisking building material up into the air to create the new Docklands city around the great empty docks.

In Woolwich Reach we could see all the modern glories of the capital. The Millennium Dome, the Canary Wharf Tower and in the far distance the London Eye wheel. We swept up river towards the elegance of Greenwich and the tea clipper *Cutty Sark,* sitting majestically in her permanent berth. The *Cutty Sark's* bowsprit end had been the finishing mark for two Thames Races we had taken part in with *L'Atalanta.* In 1973 the barges and gaff class had made an anchor start at Greenhithe and we had finished 6th in the gaff class. In the evening we had gone ashore for the prize giving. Seventy-nine-year old Mrs Dorothea Woodward Fisher, 'Old Mother Thames', had presented the prizes and given all the prize-winners a kiss. This was after Dolly Fisher had made a rousing speech, in her crisp Edwardian upper class English, demanding that more should be done to protect the commercial activities on the London River.

Even in 1973 the docking system of the upper Port of London was already almost dead, but Dolly Fisher had spent her life fighting for commercial barge traffic on the River and she was not going to give up. The up-river Port of London had been barge dominated, both sailing and dumb barges, because of a wording written into the first Dock Act. This allowed a barge to go into the docks and be loaded over the side of a ship without paying any dues. The handling of the dumb barges, which in the early days were rowed on the tide, was a 'closed shop' and could only be done by lightermen who had served an apprentice-ship and belonged to their union.

Dolly Fisher, who came from a comfortable middle class family, had defied the conventions of her day by marrying Billy Woodward Fisher, a London River lighterman. She was the only woman on the old London River to get a lighterman's licence. She used to go off on the tideway with a barge, smoking a clay pipe and wearing a pin-striped suit. Dolly and her husband started the firm of W.N. Woodward Fisher and their first craft was an old wooden lighter that cost them £20. They were based at Molassine Wharf, Greenwich and there was a Barge Repair Yard nearby at Morden Wharf. At its peak in 1950, W.N. Woodward Fisher had 125 dumb barges (the steel swim-headed lighters) and eleven tugs working on the Thames.

Like most of the London River lighterage firms, Woodward Fisher finished up in debt; however when Dolly Fisher sold up her last barges they were 'blacked' by the watermen. No one would touch them because her lightermen demanded 'a dab in a dook', a lighter-man's slang word for a back-hander or more politely, golden handshake. Dolly felt that she had found good jobs for all of them but they said she lived in a big house and should pay up. Dolly Fisher did not budge on this matter, but it was the sort of row that helped to kill the trade on the old London River.

As well as being actively engaged in running the barge firm, Dolly Fisher did a great deal of charity work, and raised the money to build a new clubhouse for the Poplar Rowing Club, for which she was awarded an OBE. When she died, Bill Lungley of the Transport Union said: 'In spite of our differences and arguments, I had the greatest respect for Dolly and admired her attitude to the Thames.' For a union man on the Thames to make such a remark about an employer was the highest praise anyone could ever get.

As we reached Greenwich in the *Crangon* we passed Pope and Bond's barge repair yard, one the few remaining, but it looked empty, waiting perhaps for some property developer to remodel it as a waterside residence. Out in the tideway some rusty old barges lay in the 'lighter roads'. At one time the upper Thames seemed to be much narrower because it was lined with lighter roads. The Thames watermen have kept alive the art of rowing a barge on the tideway by holding a series of races, but by 2000 the river had become a totally different place compared to the old working river.

We felt a real sense of achievement as we locked *Crangon* into St Katharine's Dock just below Tower Bridge. The harbour master looked down on the tiny wooden Yarmouth shrimper, sandwiched between sleek German and Dutch yachts, and asked 'are you going home tonight?' We were surprised and said 'no, why do you ask? ' 'Well', he said, 'there is nowhere to sleep on there'. He was almost right, the *Crangon* is not a comfortable boat to sleep aboard, but at £17 a night for three people to sleep in the centre of London at least it was cheap.

Before leaving to return to the River Deben, we found Hays' barge *Cabby* and had a chat with Gerard Swift, the skipper, who took charter parties on the Thames. Two months later Pearl and I joined the *Cabby* at Butler's Wharf, just below Tower Bridge. In the summer

The *Crangon* alongside the steel sailing barge *Wyvenhoe*, waiting to lock into St Katharine's Dock near Tower Bridge, 2000.

the Pool of London is constantly churned up by the endless wash from passing tripper boats with their loudspeakers giving the passengers lively, but questionable, accounts of English history. In the autumn the Pool was much quieter, with the occasional barge going up under Tower Bridge.

In the strong tide, the *Cabby* tugged at her mooring ropes. A great deal of money had been spent on this barge and she was in beautiful condition. Forty years before, most of the wooden barges had looked worn out by decades of cargo-carrying, but by 2000 some, like the *Cabby, Mirosa* and *May,* had been returned to as good as new condition.

We were taking a party of councillors from Rainham down river to have a look at their borough from the water. None of them had seen it from the river before. For Gerard Swift, this was an easy trip, for he often takes the barge across to Holland and even across to southern Ireland. Gerard watched the Rainham party, rather like a shepherd counting his flock. Once the party and the lunch had been brought aboard Gerard nodded to his mate, Mark, to cast off. With a slight touch on the engine the barge moved away from the wharf. Gordon Hardy, who used to be skipper of the steel barge *Portlight,* back in the 1950s, used to say that you should come away from a wharf 'as easy as stepping on a bus', but Gerard, with his powerful engine, made it seem a lot easier than travelling by public transport.

In the days of sail a barge only made a passage when the tide was in her favour, but nowadays most barges must earn their keep by doing charter work and they have to use an engine to suit their passengers. The tide was ebbing hard and we quickly passed down the

AJ and RS on the *Crangon* in the Lower Pool of London. The Yarmouth shrimpers have a loose-footed mainsail on to which the boom is fitted. This allowed them, in the same way as the bawleys did, to control their speed while trawling under sail.

lower Pool of London. On the north shore, some of old warehouses had survived, but below Cherry Garden Pier the south shore had become a huge housing estate. On the south shore there is the Essex Buoy, which got its name because the Essex stackie barges used to lie there and lower their masts ready to be rowed up river on the tide to their discharging berths. We slid on down river past Cherry Garden Pier and the old piles that had been part of Bellamy's Wharf. The developers had wanted to pull these out, but the new residents had got up a petition to stop them removing this feature of the old working river.

On the north shore, nineteenth century houses remained but ahead of us rose the new shiny high-rise buildings on the Isle of Dogs. No area of Britain has changed more totally than the transformation of the London docks into Docklands. In Britain, basically a small island with limited space, it makes sense to build upwards with office accommodation rather than sprawling out over the limited countryside. Sadly, in the bright new world of Dockland development the new residents have been cut off from the river. A few of the old waterman's steps have survived, but there are no boats at any of them. These reaches have been carefully re-designed so that the river is just a backdrop to housing and offices, not a place that local people can use for recreation.

Lower down, below the great white elephant of the Millennium Dome, there are the moorings of the Greenwich Yacht Club, a hardy bunch of local boating people, who have sailed these waters since 1908. Down here re-development is not so advanced, the abandoned Millennium Flour Mill sat alone beside the Royal Docks while building was going on all around it.

The tide carried the *Cabby* down river and she was making 9 miles an hour over the ground. The Woolwich Reach was completely empty, even the ferry was not on the move. Gerard Swift had learnt to sail on his father's 82ft sailing barge *Dawn* at Maldon. He could just remember going to the Woolwich Buoys, to do some work on *Raybel,* where barges used to lie 'waiting for orders' to load in the docks.

I can remember being there in the 1950s and sculling the skipper ashore so that he could walk up to a little shop and see if the owners had phoned down with instructions for loading the next freight. Gone are the days when barge owners phoned the local shop to ask them to send someone down to the river's edge to shout the instructions across the water. On this trip, Gerard spent a lot of time on the mobile phone and aft, near the wheel, a ship's radio cracked away with information about shipping movements on the river. This has taken the remoteness away from seafaring.

When we were below the Gallions Reach and the old London Dock system, our party from Rainham started to take a keen interest in Dagenham, and then in the Halfway Reach, the Rainham shore. Frankly it is not very exciting, we could see the Ford Car Plant and then a container storage area and car breaker's yard.

On *Cabby's* foredeck I was told that Rainham Creek had been dammed up after the 1953 Floods. The area was pointed out at the creek mouth where there had once been a hamlet called Ferry. There had been a pub there called the 'Three Crowns' and a ferry that used to run across to Erith and back, until the Dartford Tunnel had been opened. The Ferry hamlet had completely vanished and its site was buried in a vast collection of old London buses. The Rainham party had plans, and apparently a European grant had been given, to push the clock back and create a pleasant waterside 'Heart of the Thames Gateway' leisure area beside the river.

In Erith Roads, Gerard swung the wheel and turned the barge around to go back up river with the young flood tide. The *Cabby* was a coasting barge that had been able to load 160 tons, but her present owners, Hays, have her superbly fitted out as a promotional barge. *Cabby*, like most of the barges, survived because she was large enough to be converted to a motor barge but she was converted back to a sailing barge later. The *Cabby* inherited much of her gear from the barge *Sirdar* and the carved bow rail and name board of *Sirdar* are down in the saloon.

Several times Pearl and I had followed the Medway Barge Match on the *Sirdar* and she later became the barge that did not want to die. Crescent Shipping decided to scrap the *Sirdar,* took all her sailing gear out and dumped her in Whitewall Creek on the River Medway. One high tide the *Sirdar* floated out and one of Crescent's coaster skippers suddenly found her hulk drifting down river when he was coming up in the dark. After this she was taken down the Medway to another creek, but again she floated out and finally a tug was sent down to smash up the hulk. This was a sad and perhaps pointless end for a fine barge.

The *Sirdar* is not the only spritty barge I had sailed on which has become a hulk or even been completely broken up. When I sailed on the *Spinaway C, Memory, Millie, Lord Roberts, Convoy* and *Redoubtable* they all seemed very sound and permanent, but none of them are left afloat. I also sailed on the Maldon stackie barge *Dawn*, when she was skippered by Gordon Swift, and another time when Gerard was skipper. Ten years later, when the *Dawn* had become an unrigged hull in a Kent boatyard, Gordon set out to try and save her.

The plan was to bring *Dawn* back to Maldon, where she had been built in 1897. Since the previous owners had only rebuilt one side, the Holdsworth brothers, Neil and Stuart, offered to put her in a portable dry dock. They gave the 120ft (36.58m) Dutch coaster *Johno*, which was sunk in a Medway creek and *Dawn* was floated above her hold and settled down on blocks in *Johno* as the tide fell. At low water the *Johno* was made watertight again and on the following tide she was refloated, with *Dawn* happily sitting in the hold. After this they were towed back to Maldon. All that had to be done after that was to find somebody to help finance the rest of the rebuild, which sounds easy if you say it quickly.

A cool afternoon breeze blew across the river and we hurried back up river in the *Cabby* and came alongside the pier at Tower Bridge. All these trips around the coast of south-eastern England had started as dreams, then became reality but in the end, memories last longer than dreams.

Gordon Swift on the coaster *Johno* just after her arrival at Maldon, 1998. The sailing barge *Dawn* is in the background, in *Johno's* hold.

GLOSSARY

BALTIC TRADER. Vessel built to carry cargo in the Baltic. Almost always wooden. Two types, the klipperbygget (clipper built) with a clipper bow and counter stern and the jagt-bygget (yachtbuilt) or Marstal-built hulls with flat sloping transom stern and a round bow. The ketches were known as galeases. Many were sold to British owners between 1960 and 1987.

BARGE YACHT. A yacht, usually gaff rigged, built with flat bottom and sides similar to a Thames sailing barge.

BAWLEY. Technically a smack, but they were seldom called this. They were gaff cutters with a loose-footed mainsail which could be brailed up to control their speed when trawling. After coppers were fitted to boil the catch on the way home they became 'boiler boats' which seems to have been corrupted into bawley. Although in some places, such as Pin Mill, their name 'boiler boats' was used until modern times.

BE-NEAPED. To be trapped by the small tide and be unable to float or to leave a berth.

CARVEL. Method of building wooden boats when the outside planks are laid on top of each other so that the exterior of the hull is smooth.

CLINKER. Method of building a wooden boat with outside planks overlapping. Probably gets its name from the 'plinker' noise of the water hitting the 'lands', where planks overlap.

COUNTER STERN. The stern of a craft aft of the rudder which extends the deck out. Popular in the Victorian and Edwardian period.

FORELUG. The larger forward sail on a dipping lugger. Originally the luggers were three masted and after the mainmast was left out the larger sail still remained the forelug or foresail.

HERRING NETS. The nets we use are 33 yards (30 metres) long and six score deep. A score is twenty, so the nets with 120 meshes deep are six score. The old 'cran' measurement of herring was supposed to be 750 herring.

HUFFLER. Sometimes called a mud pilot. These were men with good local knowledge of an area, but they didn't have a pilot's licence. The East Coast term huffler came from the fact that in the London River the mud pilot used to stand forward on the sloping bow or huff of the early nineteenth century swimhead barges.

LEEBOARDS. Boards on the side of a barge, which are lowered down to help grip the water and allow the barge to sail against the wind.

LIGHTER ROADS. Buoys on which tiers of barges were moored. Originally the buoys were placed in the tideway by the Port of London Authority, so that lighter rowing barges did not have to anchor, but just lay on a buoy when the tide was no longer in their favour. Later firms stored their barges in the roads, often loaded with cargo. It was cheaper than a warehouse.

LUGGER. Boat with a four-sided sail set on a yard. On the dipping lugger the sail has to be lowered and 'shifted' to the other side of the mast when the boat changes to a fresh tack against the wind. The standing lugsail does not go forward of the mast and can remain set while tacking to windward.

MATCH. A race for sailing barges.

MULIE. A coasting spritsail barge with a gaff mizzen. A mulie because it was a cross between a boomie (gaff ketch) and a spritsail barge.

NEAP TIDES. The small tides every two weeks when the moon is waning. Comes from the Anglo-Saxon *Nepflod*. *Nep* meant 'lacking'.

QUANT. A long pole used for punting a craft on the Norfolk Broads.

SHRIMPER. Boat or fisherman involved in catching shrimp.

SMACK. The term probably comes from the German 'smuck' meaning a bluff-bowed fishing boat. The term came from the noise made by the bows as these boats hit a sea. In the eighteenth century maritime language a smack was a gaff-rigged single masted craft. The most famous of these were the Customs House smacks (Revenue cutters) and the Leith smacks which carried passengers between Edinburgh and London. From the Victorian period onwards a smack has been a decked gaff-rigged fishing boat.

SPRING TIDE. The highest tide with a full moon. Highest equinoctial tides come in the spring and autumn. The Anglo-Saxon for spring tide was *fyllepflod*. *Fyllan* meant 'to fill' while *flod* was 'to flow'. *Tyd* or tide meant 'time' and this lived on in the London River, 'tide time' meant high water.

SPRITTY. Essex and Suffolk term for a spritsail barge.

STAYSAIL BARGE. A spritsail barge without a bowsprit setting just five sails inboard. Also called a stem head rig.

STUMPY. A spritsail barge without a topmast. Usually used in the brick and cement trade between the Medway and the Thames.

SWIM-HEAD. The flat sloping bow of the London River lighters. These were always called barges by the lightermen who worked them.

WHERRY. Wherry is a term usually meaning and open rowing boat. It would appear that the fast rowing boats on the Norfolk Broads developed into decked craft used for carrying cargo. They had a single gaff sail set on a very solid mast stepped well forward in the bow to help them go against the wind.

WITHY. A branch or pole pushed into the mud to mark a channel.

YAWL. Norse word meaning a boat. On the East Coast of England and Scotland a yawl, pronounced 'yoll' in East Anglia, was usually an open lugger. In yachting terms a yawl is a two-masted craft with the mizzen stepped aft of the rudder.

Canvey Island, The Lobster Smack